CELEBRITY INSULTS

First published in Great Britain in 2009 by Prion Books

an imprint of the Carlton Publishing Group
20 Mortimer Street
London W1T 3JW

A catalogue record for this book is available from the British Library

ISBN 978-1-85375-705-1

10 9 8 7 6 5 4 3 2 1

Printed in the UK by CPI Mackays, Chatham, ME5 8TD

CELEBRITY INSULTS

Over 1,000 put-downs,
jibes and cheap shots

Edited by Michael Powell

PRION

CONTENTS

INTRODUCTION

In a *Guardian* article last year, Julie Burchill opined "bring back the red-blooded bitch", complaining that "these days, bitching is low-fat, decaffeinated and kick-free". Well, I beg to differ with the crazy old dyke (an epithet she launched at Camille Paglia with sub-zero finesse in the infamous "Fax Wars" of 1993). This book is near-libellous proof that bucketfuls of vicious bile are still being sloshed about by celebrities of both sexes and that badinage is very much alive and kicking.

An ancient Arab proverb advises that insults should be written in sand, compliments carved in stone, but for your convenience I have chosen ink and recycled paper. Mostly, I have stuck deliberately to contemporary venting of spleen. Apologies if a few of the entries are achingly banal in their lack of imagination and articulation, but I stand by them as entertaining barometers of popular culture, since they so often reveal more about the insulter than the victim and I've included a smattering of classic barbs from the likes of Bette Davies and others to show that times haven't really changed.

Some of these insults are milestones in feuding history; lots of the abuse has been scratched into the public consciousness recently and some is throwaway, quotidian invective, including dysfunctional Tweets and the envy-filled vomitus that pops up every week on

YouTube and online gossip blogs (check out Brandon Davis's odious jibes about Lindsay Lohan's private parts – with friends like these...).

During my research I couldn't help noticing that the music industry is the most prolific generator of bad mouthing, from the gritted teeth of hoary rockers to the Botoxed lips of pop princesses. At first I didn't know why. Maybe the speed with which music careers crash and burn makes for greater insecurity and raw naked bitchiness. However, sport is equally cruel and competitive, but many of the sport-related insults are only a wink away from good-natured ribbing. Maybe it's because rock stars are less inhibited, get less sleep and take more drugs than the rest of us, or that they simply have more time on their hands – lots of sitting around in hotel rooms and recording suites doing lines and ranting, instead of getting out in the fresh air to kick a ball around. Finally I solved the mystery: a disproportionate number of insults come from Boy George and Lily Allen!

Men and women seem equally capable of giving and receiving a good tongue-lashing although reading this collection you might wonder what became of sisterhood – even Germaine Greer recently described Michelle Obama's inaugural dress as a "geometrical haemorrhage". I'll leave you to judge whether the age of the great acerbic wits has long passed, or if Paris Hilton and Noel Gallagher have staked their claim as the Dorothy Parker and Oscar Wilde of the twenty-first century.

Michael Powell, 2009

ACTORS

Tom Cruise is a maniac. I can't understand
the way he conducts his life.

LAUREN BACALL

A coward, a bully, a bigmouth and
a queer-basher.

CHRISTOPHER HITCHENS on Mel Gibson

He probably has a really small penis.

MADONNA on Antonio Banderas

In his bodybuilding days Arnold Schwarzenegger was
known as the Austrian Oak. Then he started acting and
was known as... the Austrian Oak.

JACK DEE

Brad Pitt is handsome but not that talented. And he
admits he goes through four cartons of cigarettes a
week. Need I say less?

HELENA BONHAM CARTER

Anyone who says my show is "neat" has got to go.

MADONNA on Kevin Costner

I couldn't cast someone who sounds like a small Polynesian island.

TERENCE DAVIES on Keanu Reeves

You've got a mid-life crisis haircut.

JONATHAN ROSS to Tom Hanks

Brian Murphy is a naturally appalling actor. He always looks as if he has been given a premature break as his own understudy.

A. A. GILL

. . . a beached whale.

NICHOLAS DE JONGH on Tony Slattery
after he appeared on stage naked

I'm the fourth choice of host for this
part of the evening. The first choice was Nicholas
de Jongh, but he was withdrawn at the last moment
following the shock revelation that he's a c**t.

TONY SLATTERY at the Olivier Awards

Most of the time he sounds like
he has a mouth full of wet toilet paper.

REX REED on Marlon Brando

A fellow with the inventiveness of Albert Einstein but
with the attention span of Daffy Duck.

TOM SHALES on Robin Williams

He seems to think he's Lee Marvin — except he's two
feet shorter and about one third the talent.

JOHN BOORMAN on Mel Gibson

Spielberg isn't a film-maker, he's a confectioner.

ALEX COX

Tom Cruise is a midget and he has eight bodyguards, all 6ft 10in, which makes him even more diminutive. It's an absolute joke. Actors are unimportant.

RICHARD HARRIS

Quite an actor, Sean Penn. And not an asshole like Russell Crowe.

JOSH BROLIN accepting an award at a New York Film Critics Awards dinner

You are confusing your talent with the size of your paycheck.

MARLON BRANDO to Val Kilmer

Kevin Costner has personality minus.

MADONNA

The guy's forty going on twelve. I was never going to put up with his silly tantrums. And he behaves like a fucking girl. If I saw him, I wouldn't give him the time of day. If he approached me, I would stand and wait. I would be right there in front of the bloke. And I would have to resort to my old career.

JOE BUGNER on Russell Crowe

You get someone like Russell Crowe and you want to say to the camera: "He is a piece of — get ready to bleep this — fucking shit".

JOAN RIVERS on Russell Crowe live on *Loose Women*

If he wants to see *Chicago*, I've left him two tickets; one adult, one child.

BROOKE SHIELDS on Tom Cruise

Arnold Schwarzenegger looks like a condom
full of walnuts.

CLIVE JAMES

The only reason he had a child is so that he
can meet babysitters.

DAVID LETTERMAN on Warren Beatty

Steve McQueen had that look people get
when they ride in elevators.

ANATOLE BROYARD

Sean Connery's amazing array of accents includes
Russian-Scottish, Irish-Scottish, Spanish-Scottish,
Arabian-Scottish, and English-Scottish.

SIMON ROSE

He looks like a child with a lot of make up.

JESSICA ALBA on Zac Efron

Warren is a pussy… He's a wimp… I know I have a much bigger following than Warren does, and a lot of my audience isn't even aware of who he is.

MADONNA on Warren Beatty

He is to acting what Liberace was to pumping iron.

REX REED on Sylvester Stallone

When you talk about a great actor, you're not talking about Tom Cruise. His whole behaviour is so shocking. It's inappropriate and vulgar and absolutely unacceptable to use your private life to sell anything commercially, but, I think, it's kind of a sickness.

LAUREN BACALL

His features resembled a fossilized wash rag.

ALAN BRIEN on Steve McQueen

I've got three words for him: "Am. A. Teur".

CHARLIE SHEEN on Colin Farrell

Sly Stallone is five-seven, I believe. Shorter than you'd think — not just short on talent. Anyway, he only hires actors his height or shorter, unless they're to play some kind of freakish villain. So I'll never work with Stallone unless I let him shoot me, and I'll never let myself get that desperate!

BURT LANCASTER

I'll never put Tom Cruise down. He's already kinda' short.

DON SIMPSON

He has the vocal modulation of a railway-station announcer, the expressive power of a fence-post and the charisma of a week-old head of lettuce.

FINTAN O'TOOLE on Quentin Tarantino

Politically Mel Gibson is somewhere to the right of Attila the Hun. He's beautiful, but only on the outside.

SUSAN SARANDON

Well at least he's finally found his true love. What a pity he can't marry himself.

FRANK SINATRA on Robert Redford

As you know, Tom Cruise and Katie Holmes had a baby girl. It weighs seven pounds seven ounces and is twenty inches long… wait, that's Tom.

DAVID LETTERMAN

It is easy to laugh at David Hasselhoff's pomposity. But first of all you should laugh at his hair. Then you should laugh at his face, his teeth, his name, his hair again, his acting ability, his singing ability and his grasp of his place in the scheme of things.

MARK LAMARR

Tom Cruise is to hunks what Velveeta is to cheese.

EMILE ARDOLINO

A self-important, boring, flash-in-the-pan Brit.

ROBERT DOWNEY JR. on Hugh Grant

Tom Cruise and Nicole Kidman say their split was amicable, and they want everyone to know that after the divorce is final, their two adopted children will be returned to the prop department at Universal Studios.

TINA FEY

He's so cheap, he likes to watch porno movies
backwards so he can see the hustler giving
back the money.

JOHN BELUSHI on Billy Crystal

In order to feel safer on his private jet, John Travolta
has purchased a bomb-sniffing dog. Unfortunately for
the actor, the dog came six movies too late.

TINA FEY

Pierce Brosnan always reminds me of all
the models in men's knitwear catalogues.

PAUL HOGGART

Richard E. Grant always plays the same basic
character, simply varying the degree of intensity with
which he rolls his eyeballs.

PAUL HOGGART

Peter O'Toole has a face not so much
lived-in as infested.

PAUL TAYLOR

I don't really go for people just because they're good
looking. I mean, yes, he is gorgeous. But we all know
that he's a tramp, and I'm not going to go there.

JAMELIA on Colin Farrell

I would rather drink latex paint than be in a
movie with Steven Seagal.

HENRY ROLLINS

Peter O'Toole looks like he's walking around
just to save funeral expenses.

JOHN HUSTON

Jack Nicholson is a legend in his own lifetime
and in his own mind.

JENNIFER LOPEZ

Sean Connery has such a deep love of Scotland that he
refuses to use anything other than a Scottish accent no
matter what role he is taking.

GRAHAM NORTON

I find you a little wooden. How do you psyche yourself
up? Do you go into a forest and look at some trees?

DENNIS PENNIS (Paul Kaye) to Hugh Grant

Tom Cruise is to become a father. So we'll soon hear
the pitter-patter of tiny feet… as Tom rushes down to
the shop to get nappies.

JONATHAN ROSS

How does Francis Ford Coppola, one of the greatest film-makers of our time, see Keanu Reeves's work, see what we've all seen, and say, "That's what I want in my movie?" How does Bertolucci see that and say "That's my guy". Emilio and I sit around and just scratch our heads, thinking, "How did this guy get in?"

CHARLIE SHEEN

Either he didn't take his medication or he's acting.

RUSH LIMBAUGH on Michael J. Fox and his Parkinson's disease

He's the type of man who will end up dying in his own arms.

MAMIE VAN DOREN on Warren Beatty

I don't know about Brad Pitt, leaving that beautiful wife to go hold orphans for Angelina. I mean, how long is that going to last?

MICHAEL DOUGLAS

I felt I became a star only by association. We would go to the Oscars and I would think, "I'm here to support him". I felt it was my job to put on a beautiful dress and be seen and not heard.

NICOLE KIDMAN on Tom Cruise

He just needs attention, constant relentless attention. And he is jealous of anyone else who gets it. He can be charming, witty and gracious, but it is all because he needs something.

GEORGE TAKEI on William Shatner

Michael Caine can out-act, well nearly, any telephone kiosk you care to mention.

HUGH LEONARD

He has turned almost alarmingly blond — he's gone past platinum, he must be plutonium; his hair is coordinated with his teeth.

PAULINE KAEL on Robert Redford

It was like kissing the Berlin wall.

HELENA BONHAM CARTER on Woody Allen

. . . a scrawny, snivelling, whingeing grass.

STEVE McFADDEN on Adam Woodyatt (Ian Beale in *EastEnders*)

. . . nothing more than a fucking holiday camp redcoat.

STEVE McFADDEN on Shane Richie (Alfie Moon in *EastEnders*)

Someone thought I was Tom from the back. I guess I'd better wear heels.

SELMA BLAIR on Tom Cruise

Whatever happened to John Travolta? I heard he either joined some cult and got fat; or he married and had a child, which amounts to the same thing.

GÉRARD DEPARDIEU

His favourite exercise is climbing tall people.

PHYLLIS DILLER on Mickey Rooney

Allowing a gormless oaf like Martin Clunes to drone
Leonard Rossiter's snappy rejoinder was like letting
Peter Andre do the "don't mention the war" sketch from
Fawlty Towers. It was a travesty.

JIM SHELLEY on *The Fall & Rise of Reginald Perrin*

Nobody thought Mel Gibson could play a Scot but look
at him now: alcoholic and a racist!

FRANKIE BOYLE

Well the trailer for *Rocky Balboa* was released this week
and this movie promises to be the most
recent Rocky movie ever.

PAUL F. TOMPKINS

ACTRESSES

I'd kill myself if I was as fat as Marilyn Monroe.

ELIZABETH HURLEY

It scares me when you think Goldie Hawn probably has the best plastic surgeon in the whole world and she still looks like a fish that's being pushed through a keyhole.

GRAHAM NORTON

Don't worry, honey, you'll grow into your nose one day.

ANJELICA HUSTON to Sofia Coppola

It's been reported that Lindsay Lohan recently attended an Alcoholics Anonymous meeting. Lohan wasn't planning on attending the meeting — but when she woke up, that's where she'd parked.

CONAN O'BRIEN

Thank you for photograph. I do not know who this boy is.

BORAT on Lindsay Lohan

Life is for living, enjoy it while you can. Poor Mischa Barton looks so thin and she's only a young girl.

YASMIN LE BON

. . . a big old lump with too much lipstick.

STEVE McFADDEN on Jessie Wallace (Kat Moon in *EastEnders*). . .

. . . a nobody who thinks she's queen bee.

STEVE McFADDEN on Wendy Richards (Pauline Fowler in *EastEnders*)

Jerry is about to bring her timber-clad acting talents to yet another production of *The Vagina Monologues* and one is tempted to remark that this is indeed about the only part of her which might have an interesting story to tell, were it able to speak for itself.

ROD LIDDLE on Jerry Hall

This silly woman makes even Jade Goody look like someone with an Oxford first.

ANN WIDDECOMBE on Marion Cotillard

Thank you to all the perverts who voted for me.

JESSICA ALBA accepting a Golden Popcorn trophy for her sexy striptease in *Sin City*, at the MTV Movie Awards

Do I think she's a great actress? No.
Acting is what I do.

JENNIFER LOPEZ on Madonna

Reese Witherspoon. She's a dick…
What a fucking douchebag.
KEVIN SMITH

Life is difficult enough without Meryl Streep movies.
And she looks like a chicken.
TRUMAN CAPOTE

Dark hair makes her look like an old donkey that
needs to be euthanized.
PEREZ HILTON on Sarah Jessica Parker

I can't wait until Lindsay Lohan goes to jail. "Boo hoo
hoo. I'm going to jail." Good. Does that mean you'll
stop showing me your pussy now?
LILY ALLEN

Nicole Kidman's forehead looks like a fucking flatscreen
TV! How big is that forehead?
SHARON OSBOURNE

Kissing her was like kissing Hitler.
TONY CURTIS on Marilyn Monroe

She was good at being inarticulately abstracted for the same reason that midgets are good at being short.
CLIVE JAMES on Marilyn Monroe

. . . serious mental problems.
JOHN VOIGHT on his daughter Angelina Jolie

She looks like a boiled horse.
JEREMY CLARKSON on Sarah Jessica Parker

Angelina Jolie and her vacuous hubby Brad Pitt make about forty million dollars a year in violent psychopathic movies and give away three of it to starving children trying to look as if they give a crap about humanity as they spit out more dunces that will consume more than their fair share and wreck the earth even more.
ROSEANNE BARR

Scarlett is a bloody c**t.

**LINDSAY LOHAN on Scarlett Johansson (with permanent marker in a
New York bathroom stall)**

Couldn't they at least cast a real actress?

**FAYE DUNAWAY on Hilary Duff's casting in the
remake of *Bonnie and Clyde***

I think that my fans that are gonna' go see the movie
don't even know who she is… I think it was a little
unnecessary, but I might be mad if I looked
like that now, too.

HILARY DUFF on Faye Dunaway

Glenda Jackson has a face to launch a
thousand dredgers.

JACK DEMANIO

I never saw what was so great about Natalie. She was short and lousy in bed.

STEVE McQUEEN on Natalie Wood

A lot has changed. You can end up looking like a startled chimpanzee.

RUSSELL CROWE on Sharon Stone and cosmetic surgery

She has an insipid double chin, her legs are too short, and she has a slight pot-belly.

RICHARD BURTON on Elizabeth Taylor

She turned down the role of Helen Keller because she couldn't remember the lines.

JOAN RIVERS on Bo Derek

The best time I ever had with Joan Crawford was when I pushed her down the stairs in *Whatever Happened to Baby Jane?*

BETTE DAVIS

. . . no talent crackhead.

LINDSAY LOHAN on Sienna Miller

. . . flat, shallow, cardboard cut-out of an actress.

LINDSAY LOHAN on Keira Knightley

Why am I so good at playing bitches? I think it's because I'm not a bitch. Maybe that's why Miss Crawford always plays ladies.

BETTE DAVIS

When a former *EastEnders* star says they're off to Hollywood, it means Hollywood nightclub in Romford.

SUE CARROLL on Martine McCutcheon

Meryl Streep can act Polish or English or Australian but she sure as hell can't act blonde.

JOAN BENNETT

There may be a heaven, but if Joan Crawford
is there, I'm not going.
BETTE DAVIS

Look at Cher. One more face lift and she'll be
wearing a beard.
JENNIFER SAUNDERS

"Civilians" is a term I love. It's what Elizabeth Hurley
used to describe people who weren't on TV.
ALAN CARR

Looks like she was dressed by a colour blind circus
clown, and when it comes to fashion, it's chaos when
Cameron's back in town.
RICHARD BLACKWELL on Cameron Diaz

Dramatic art in her opinion is knowing how
to fill a sweater.
BETTE DAVIS on Jayne Mansfield

She resembles a tattered toothpick
trapped in a hurricane.
RICHARD BLACKWELL on Mary Kate Olsen

A painted pumpkin on a pogo stick.
RICHARD BLACKWELL on Rene Zellweger

The first time I saw Cher, I thought she was a hooker.
RONNIE SPECTOR

Joan ended the tour [of the play *Legends*, with Linda
Evans] with a sprained knee, a scar on her hand and
almost choked to death.
JOAN COLLIN'S spokesman

Some people get hot by association. I swear to God,
I don't remember anything she was in. I heard more
about her and Brad Pitt than I ever heard
about her work.
JENNIFER LOPEZ on Gwyneth Paltrow

She needs the work, and for God's sake, she's never been on stage at all — and she wasn't even that good on TV!

JOAN COLLINS on Linda Evans

Joan always cries a lot. Her tear ducts must be close to her bladder.

BETTE DAVIS on Joan Crawford

Joan Collins is the single most unprofessional actress working in Hollywood.

LINDA EVANS

I'm like Jennifer Aniston. I pick the wrong guys.

ANNE HATHAWAY

Say what you like… I've never dated con men or criminals.

JENNIFER ANISTON on Anne Hathaway

All my life I wanted to look like Liz Taylor. Now I find
that Liz Taylor is beginning to look like me.

DIVINE

Sarah Brightman couldn't act scared on the New York
subway at four o'clock in the morning.

JOEL SEGAL

I didn't know her well, but after watching her in action
I didn't want to know her well.

JOAN CRAWFORD on Judy Garland

Pamela Anderson revealed all the taste and refinement
of a hooker on holiday.

JOAN COLLINS

The greatest privacy bleater in showbusiness is Liz Hurley. Not a week goes by without this poor little lamb moaning about the appalling media intrusion into the pampered multi-millionaire lifestyle she has built on the back of a magnificently impressive lack of discernible talent.

PIERS MORGAN

They can have all the money in the world but they've got no class.

JORDAN on Elizabeth Hurley

She speaks five languages and can't act in any of them.

JOHN GIELGUD on Ingrid Bergman

Liz Hurley longs for the day when people stop pointing cameras at her. Speaking as someone who has seen all her films, I couldn't agree more.

JONATHAN ROSS

Working with Cher was like being in a blender
with an alligator.

PETER BOGDANOVITCH

Jamie Lee Curtis has trouble learning her lines
because English is not her first language. She doesn't,
unfortunately, have a first language.

JOHN CLEESE

Last month Catherine Zeta Jones raised a few eyebrows
with her flirty behaviour with veteran actor Sean
Connery, a man old enough to be her husband.

MARTIN CLUNES

Jodie Foster is very, very, very bossy. And then some.

ROBERT DOWNEY JR.

Julia Roberts is very big-mouthed. Literally, physically, she has a very big mouth. When I was kissing her, I was aware of a faint echo.

HUGH GRANT

Instead of sneaking in, if you want to be a US citizen, do it the right way. Have Angelina Jolie adopt you.

JIMMY KIMMEL

Lindsay Lohan is in rehab. She's getting her rehab out of the way before she's legally old enough to drink.

JIMMY KIMMEL

It was so warm today that Angelina Jolie adopted Ben & Jerry.

DAVID LETTERMAN

A lucky model who's been given a lot of opportunities.
JENNIFER LOPEZ on Cameron Diaz

The Russians love Brooke Shields because her eyebrows
remind them of Leonid Brezhnev.
ROBIN WILLIAMS

In Hollywood she's revered, she gets nominated for
Oscars, but I've never heard anyone in the public or
among my friends say, "Oh, I love Winona Ryder".
JENNIFER LOPEZ

I think it's great. Obviously to him, age doesn't matter,
and to her, size doesn't matter.
BRITTANY MURPHY on Demi Moore and Ashton Kutcher

Would you ever consider keeping your clothes on if the
script demanded it?
DENNIS PENNIS (Paul Kaye) to Demi Moore

I saw Angelina Jolie on TV. Those lips are so big, she could whisper in her own ear.

JOAN RIVERS

Gwyneth Paltrow is quite pretty in a British, horsey sort of way.

JULIA ROBERTS

She's like an apple turnover that got crushed in a grocery bag on a hot day.

CAMILLE PAGLIA on Drew Barrymore

She lives in rarified air that's a little thin. It's like she's not getting quite enough oxygen.

SHARON STONE on Gwyneth Paltrow

They'd have to pay me an awful lot of money to work with James Cameron again.

KATE WINSLET

She doesn't understand the history of
psychiatry... I do.
**TOM CRUISE on Brooke Shields taking drugs for her
postpartum depression**

I mean, don't ask me what happened with Renee
Zellweger. I don't know how you get married
for four months.
MICHAEL DOUGLAS

Make a sex tape and grow up.
JAMIE FOXX on Miley Cyrus

It's a new low for actresses when you have to wonder
what's between her ears instead of her legs.
KATHERINE HEPBURN on Sharon Stone

Gorgeous face, garish taste…what a waste.
MR BLACKWELL on Eva Longoria

She's in *Quantum of Solace* next, the new Bond movie.
Good move, otherwise she'd get stuck in the past,
bonnet-cast, as Keira Knightley has done.
SAM WOLLASTON on Gemma Arterton

Angelina Jolie's lips are like an infected arsehole.
JOAN RIVERS

ARTS & LITERATURE

Complete loose-stool-water. Arse-gravy of the very worst kind.

STEPHEN FRY on Dan Brown's novel, *The Da Vinci Code*

What a clogged-up, clod-hopping, plate-juggling great show-off he is.

JULIE BURCHILL on Martin Amis

I went on Amazon and I bought six Jeremy Clarkson books, which you must never do because it will change your Amazon customer profile in a way that can take literally thousands of man hours to correct.

STEWART LEE

Have you heard Brian Sewell, the art critic? I bet even the Queen laughs at his accent.

PAUL MERTON

He's an idiot, like a big cheesecake on legs.
BOY GEORGE on Andy Warhol

Ignorant, inarticulate, talentless, loutish.
BRIAN SEWELL on Tracey Emin

It is no more interesting than a stuffed pike over a pub door. Indeed there may well be more art in a stuffed pike than a dead sheep.
BRIAN SEWELL on Damien Hirst's pickled sheep

I loved Lucian without liking him and there came a point where love was too painful and the dislike sufficient to say it really would be more sensible to end this relationship.
CLEMENT FREUD on his brother Lucian Freud

Anyone who has ever met Emin knows that she couldn't
think her way out of a paper bag.

IVAN MASSOW on Tracey Emin

Is it possible to be a good conceptual artist and also
very stupid? There's no hope for Tracey Emin.
She's just no good.

PHILIP HENSHER

He's pervy and creepy… I don't want to spend the next
year suing some little tosser, but I feel
very upset about this.

TRACEY EMIN on Philip Hensher

[Her] insights were, and remain, negligible, on the
level of a toddler having a tantrum.

MICHAEL BYWATER on Julie Burchill

The problem in this case is some of Oprah's picks. She's picked some good books, but she's picked enough schmaltzy, one dimensional ones that I cringe, myself, even though I think she's really smart and she's really fighting the good fight.

JONATHAN FRANZEN after his book *The Corrections* became a club selection

Those who can't teach, write. Those who can't write, write about themselves — in Toby's case, endlessly.

GRAYDON CARTER on Toby Young

Those who can't teach, write. Those who can't write employ someone to write for them and then pass it off as their own work.

TOBY YOUNG on Graydon Carter

Incredible for us – having Germaine Greer here. You are of course, both famous and celebrated for your work. On *Celebrity Big Brother 3*.

SIMON AMSTELL

What a truly disgusting sack of shit Hitchens is.

ALEXANDER COCKBURN on Christopher Hitchens

She needs open-heart surgery, and they should go in through her feet.

JULIE ANDREWS on columnist Joyce Haber

You've got a wop name, so you think you're Robert De Niro… I'm not as loud as you, but if push comes to shove I'm nastier. I'm ten years younger, two stone heavier, and I haven't had my nuts taken off by academia.

JULIE BURCHILL to Camille Paglia

You and your coterie seem to have the mental age of undergraduates, with whom I am certainly used to dealing. What empty bluster and tired clichés! If you were once witty, I'm afraid you're in a bit of a decline. I have no idea who you are.

CAMILLE PAGLIA to Julie Burchill

Dear Professor Paglia,
Fuck off you crazy old dyke.
Always,

JULIE BURCHILL

The "g" is silent – the only thing about her that is.

JULIE BURCHILL on Camille Paglia

. . . a fat bird in a blue mac sitting in the corner [at the Groucho Club].

DEBORAH BOSELEY on Julie Burchill

Andy Warhol is the only genius I've ever known with an IQ of 60.

GORE VIDAL

. . . peeled quail's egg dipped in celery salt.

PRIVATE EYE **on Toby Young**

CELEBRITY
CHEFS

Gordon Ramsay has a dried-up riverbed for a face.

TANYA GOLD

Gordon Ramsay's recent perma-tan was going too far –
I think he's slightly disappeared up the LA backside.

PIERS MORGAN

Ainsley's not a chef, he's a fucking comedian.

GORDON RAMSAY on Ainsley Harriott

I ate in Nick's restaurant and the only fucking
memorable thing was the carpets.

GORDON RAMSAY on Nick Nairn

I would rather have food at my four-year-old daughter's
prep school than at Quaglino's.

GORDON RAMSAY on Sir Terence Conran

I can eat food as good as his from the
Heinz baby range.

SIR TERENCE CONRAN on Gordon Ramsay

I hate Gary Rhodes's programmes and I think that
Antony Worrall Thompson is worse. He is dreadful, just
repulsive. I think that *Food and Drink*, the show that he
is on, is the most disgusting programme on television.
I will never, ever know, as long as I live, how the BBC or
the general public can tolerate it.

DELIA SMITH

. . . the Volvo of cooking, reliable but dull.

ANTONY WORRALL THOMPSON on Delia Smith

I couldn't give a fuck what that jumped-up little French
twat thinks. The only reason he's in Britain is because
he failed in France. When I heard Maison Blanc had
gone tits up, it added two inches to my cock.

GORDON RAMSAY on Raymond Blanc

Sexy... but only from the neck up.

GORDON RAMSAY on Nigella Lawson

... a squashed Bee Gee.

GORDON RAMSAY on Antony Worrall Thompson

If someone doesn't enrich my life, I don't want them to be part of my life. He has nothing to contribute to it.

MARCO PIERRE WHITE on Gordon Ramsay

Here we are trying to establish a reputation across the world for this country's food and along comes Delia and tips it out of a can. That hurts.

GORDON RAMSAY on Delia Smith

The reason why Jamie Oliver is so alive in people's consciousness is the same reason why Geri Halliwell is alive in people's consciousness, why Ronan Keating is alive in people's consciousness, why Lulu can make a comeback. They're all vacuous two-dimensional nonentities. We get the government we deserve and the celebrities we deserve.

KEITH ALLEN

A wonderful chef, but a really second-rate human being.

A. A. GILL on Gordon Ramsay

The darling of the blue-rinse brigade.

GORDON RAMSAY on Jamie Oliver

I don't like to speak about Tana's cooking. It gives me indigestion.

GORDON RAMSAY on his wife

French women are awkward, stinky and can't drive. I once had a French girlfriend. It was like going to bed with a Rottweiler on your chest.

GORDON RAMSAY

If I was in charge, I'd get rid of Jamie Oliver and tell people to eat what they liked.

BORIS JOHNSON

If I never speak to that guy again for the rest of my life, it wouldn't bother me one bit. Wouldn't give a fuck… sad bastard.

MARCUS WAREING on former mentor Gordon Ramsay

COMEDY

When we're together and she's in her heels, I always feel like Tom Cruise next to Nicole Kidman.

**ELLEN DEGENERES on walking the red carpet
with girlfriend Portia de Rossi**

Graham Norton is a baboon in mascara.

TANYA GOLD

We're all basing this on what Stephen Hawking said and the fact is, he's subject to interference from minicabs.

JEREMY HARDY

His idea of wit is a barrage of filth and the kind of humour most men grow out of in their teens.

ANN WIDDECOMBE on Jimmy Carr

I never thought he was a racist. I just thought he was
a fat, white bastard.

TREVOR McDONALD on Bernard Manning

I did have a dreadful mother. Isn't that a terrible thing
to say? But it's true. She was classically self-centred.
Always thought entirely of herself. And she lived to 101
– I thought I'd never get rid of her.

JOHN CLEESE

I could never compete with Sarah Silverman. I will
never be able to say the word vagina as many
times as she can.

RAINN WILSON

You can read Russell Brand's autobiography and
dismiss it as rubbish if you like, or you can dismiss it
as rubbish without reading it, to save time,
if you'd prefer.

STEWART LEE

Roseanne went on *Saturday Night Live* and said I had a 3-inch penis. Well, even a 747 looks small if it's landing in the Grand Canyon.

TOM ARNOLD

I'm not upset about my divorce. I'm only upset that I'm not a widow.

ROSEANNE BARR on Tom Arnold

Ian Hislop looks rather like King Edward – the potato not the monarch.

PAUL MERTON

He doesn't have a tiny penis; it looks small next to his gigantic balls… Jimmy's balls smell exactly like my nana's house: Benson and Hedges Deluxe Ultra Lights and brisket. God I miss her.

SARAH SILVERMAN on Jimmy Kimmel

Frankie Howerd's wig looked as if it had its
own dandruff.

NANCY BANKS-SMITH

Sylvester Stallone's mother's plastic surgery looks so
bad it could have been bought through a
mail order catalogue.

GRAHAM NORTON

Steve Martin has basically one joke and he's it.

DAVE FELTON

The closest thing to Roseanne Barr's singing the
national anthem was my cat being neutered.

JOHNNY CARSON

I have to say that Frank Skinner has never, ever, ever made me laugh – ever! He's just never, ever, ever, ever, made me laugh. The amount of money he has earned for not making me laugh is staggering!

WILL SELF on Frank Skinner

An elaborately coiffured scrotum.

LINDA SMITH on Lionel Blair

Jennifer Saunders is a one-trick horse; Dawn French is a one-trick carthorse.

A. A. GILL

"Hi Ho Silver Lining" has ruined more wedding receptions than Phil being first in line at the buffet.

MARK LAMARR on Phil Jupitus

Most comedians aren't funny in real life. Take Jennifer – she's so boring if you meet her. Her natural state is flatlining.

RUBY WAX on Jennifer Saunders

He started out as an alternative comedian, railing against Thatcherism and the like, and now earns a fortune writing the librettos for truly awful West End musicals. I mean, his name has become a byword for shameless hackery. He's the biggest sell-out of his generation.

TOBY YOUNG on Ben Elton

Peter Kay… helped me out when he released his new DVD 'cos I really needed a Christmas present for someone really thick that I hate.

SIMON AMSTELL

Ruby Wax talks like a cement mixer from Brooklyn.

DAVID NAUGHTON

What happened to proper magic? When you see a magician you wanna go "I wonder how he did that?" not "what a prick!"

JASON MANFORD on David Blaine's endurance stunts

I used to hate David Copperfield till he [David Blaine] came along. Now I quite miss the spangly blow-dried ponce.

SEAN LOCK

I used to love Michael Jackson, but now I think he's just a pale imitation of the man he used to be.

JIMMY CARR

I think that Russell Brand looks like Dot Cotton in a cat suit.

SEAN LOCK

FASHION

Fuck those two posh old tarts. I looked like Ann Widdecombe's younger, not so attractive, sister.

JO BRAND on Trinny Woodall and Susannah Constantine

I like David Beckham. Most of us have skeletons in our closet. But he takes his out in public.

ANDREW LAWRENCE

If I was alive when Reubens was painting, I'd have been the supermodel and Kate Moss would have been the paintbrush.

DAWN FRENCH

Just watched *The Wrestler*, loved it, I wouldnt be surprised if Donatella Versace goes on to win the Oscar. She was amazing.

ALAN CARR (on Twitter)

Posh doesn't strike me as particularly stylish. I don't
think she's a good example of British style at all.

MISCHA BARTON on Victoria Beckham

I've got much more style than Jordan. I don't just go
out in a bra and knickers and I don't think
I dress like a tart.

JODIE MARSH

Victoria Beckham? Does this tampon make me look fat?

JOAN RIVERS

Now they copy me, tomorrow they will learn.

**GIORGIO ARMANI accusing Domenico Dolce & Stefano Gabbana of
stealing one of his designs – quilted trousers**

We surely have plenty to learn, but certainly not
from him… The Armani style was never a source
of inspiration for us, and it is years since we have
bothered to watch his collections.

DOMENICO DOLCE & STEFANO GABBANA

Quite frankly, I've never understood what Mick Jagger saw in that bucktoothed Texas nag. There are a thousand home-grown Texas drag queens who could do Jerry Hall better than she does herself.

CAMILLE PAGLIA

Jordan doesn't need a fashion designer, she needs a structural engineer.

FRANK SKINNER

She looks like she combs her hair with an egg-beater.

LOUELLA PARSONS on Joan Collins

How this stroppy, pinch-faced little coke-snorter from Croydon ever made it to become the world's No. 1 supermodel is quite beyond me.

PIERS MORGAN on Kate Moss

Victoria Beckham gives away all her old clothes to starving children. Well, who else are they going to fit?

STEVE COOGAN

Victoria's obviously decided to exercise and not to eat
and the result is that her clothes wear her
rather than the other way around.

JANET STREET-PORTER on Victoria Beckham

It's been reported that Kate Moss recently warned
Lindsay Lohan about the danger of drugs. Moss's exact
words were, "Stay away from my drugs!"

CONAN O'BRIEN

A feminist of the younger school… fuck-me shoes and
three fat inches of cleavage… So much lipstick
must rot the brain.

GERMAINE GREER on Suzanne Moore

Who died and made Rachel Hunter a model? If I drag
up I'm more attractive.

JONATHAN ROSS

I don't get his clothes. I just don't get it. I don't get the
pushed-up sleeves, the luminescent ties.

DAVID LETTERMAN on Jay Leno

I think the only big bosoms he's interested in
are his own.

MARCELLO MASTROIANNI on Fabio

Rat-faced council estate escapee... A uniquely
unpleasant individual with appalling taste in men. Or
should that be taste in appalling men?

IAN O'DOHERTY on Kate Moss

Janet Street-Porter had the great good fortune to be
born with looks that were exactly right for her era.
When she left home in 1967, her resemblance to Plug
in *The Beano*'s Bash Street Kids was, for the first time
ever, enormously fashionable.

CHRISTOPHER HART

Kate was curled up into a little ball, writhing and
shaking and guzzling greedily from a bottle of
champagne. She looked tiny, pimply, wide-eyed, and
had a nose like Danniella Westbrook's.

PIERS MORGAN on Kate Moss

I don't hate Victoria Beckham, I just think she gives a bad image to young children. No one should be that skinny. I don't care how much she says that's her natural weight. That's just bullshit.

LILY ALLEN

I feel for Victoria. She's always in the press and wears child sizes even though she's a grown woman. It's sick. Have some food.

SARAH HARDING on Victoria Beckham

Victoria Beckham looks like a Pepperoni with two big boobies stuck on it. She's even the same colour.

IAN HYLAND

She just appeared to be the pure personification of celebrity evil: a hard-faced, arrogant creature who seemed to revel in treating everyone she dated, met or worked with, like dirt.

PIERS MORGAN on Naomi Campbell

It has been reported that Spain is the number one consumer of cocaine in the world. Apparently Spain narrowly beat Kate Moss.

CONAN O'BRIEN

That's the kind of face you hang on your door in Africa.

JOAN RIVERS on Donatella Versace

A carthorse in a badly fitting bin liner.

CAROL VORDERMAN on Susannah Constantine

An anorexic transvestite.

CAROL VORDERMAN on Trinny Woodall

Trinny is thin with very short legs, no boobs… she's as flat as a prairie.

SUSANNAH CONSTANTINE on Trinny Woodall

Who the fuck are they? They're not even in fashion.

KATE MOSS on Tom Cruise and Katie Holmes

RELIGION

& POLITICS

I think Tony Blair is better looking than him actually.
HARRIET HARMAN on Michael Sheen

It's Gordon… Gordon Ramsay?
PARIS HILTON, asked to name Britain's Prime Minister

He says he works out because it clears his mind.
Sometimes just a little too much.
JAY LENO on George W Bush

You are the deals-on-wheels Prime Minister — no
wonder the Chancellor is not a happy eater.
MICHAEL HOWARD on Tony Blair

She was a fanatic, a fundamentalist, and a fraud.
CHRISTOPHER HITCHENS on Mother Teresa

She's a twat. I would like to punch her. She is so full
of shit. She's in Kabbalah one minute; she's a Catholic
the next? She'll be a Hindu soon no doubt.
Fuck off you twat.
SHARON OSBOURNE on Madonna

I think it is typical of her to be part of an organisation
that buys God, as she doesn't like queuing
like the rest of us.

BOY GEORGE on Madonna and the Kabbalah

Just how can we see this Cabinet twice-reject, this
Brussels blow-in, this greased porker made a lord and
not, ourselves, squeal with disgust?... Poor Foy to have
acquired a baron of such medieval villainy.

QUENTIN LETTS on Peter Mandelson

Dear Tony, I have become a Communist. Enjoy
the smooze comrade.

**DAMON ALBARN rejecting an invitation to Labour's 1997 victory
reception at Downing Street**

Kissing Edwina Currie was like kissing a can opener.

GODFREY BARKER

It is ludicrously easy to knock Mrs Thatcher. It's the easiest and most obvious thing in the world to remark that she is a shameful, putrid scab, an embarrassing, ludicrous monstrosity that makes one frankly ashamed to be British, and that her ideas and standards are a stain on our national history.

STEPHEN FRY

Well John, let me put it this way. I've got a large bucket of shit lying on my desk and tomorrow morning I'm going to pour it all over your head.

KELVIN MACKENZIE to John Major

In England we have this one-eyed Scottish idiot, the one-eyed Scottish man, he keeps telling us everything's fine and he's saved the world and we know he's lying, but he's smooth at telling us.

JEREMY CLARKSON on Gordon Brown

What makes him think a middle aged actor, who's played with a chimp, could have a future in politics?

RONALD REAGAN on Clint Eastwood

She is like everything gross about a pageant
contestant, but without the desire for world peace.

SARAH SILVERMAN on Sarah Palin

By denying the responsibility of man in global warming,
by advocating gun rights and making statements
that are disconcertingly stupid, you are a disgrace to
women and you alone represent a terrible threat, a true
environmental catastrophe.

BRIGITTE BARDOT to Sarah Palin

. . . an embarrassment.

SARAH PALIN on Barack Obama

You can put lipstick on a pig. It's still a pig.

BARACK OBAMA on Sarah Palin

With Tony Blair it really was like trying to nail jelly to
the wall. In contrast, with Gordon Brown, the jelly's
already stuck to the wall. It is just a question of taking
aim at it.

WILLIAM HAGUE

And now, to make matters worse, they [the Tories] have elected a foetus as party leader.

TONY BANKS on William Hague

Making Blair peace envoy for the Middle East is like putting Mel Gibson in charge of a holocaust museum.

JOAN RIVERS

If you gave Jerry Falwell an enema, you could bury him in a matchbox.

CHRISTOPHER HITCHENS on Jerry Falwell,

the day after his death

He needs to do something about those skinny legs. We're going to make him do some squats, and then we're going to go give him some bicep curls to beef up those scrawny little arms.

ARNOLD SCHWARZENEGGER on Barack Obama

Europeans think Americans are fat, vulgar, greedy, stupid, ambitious, and ignorant, and so on. And they've taken as their own, as their representative American, someone who actually embodies all of those qualities.

CHRISTOPHER HITCHENS on Michael Moore

I was there, it was a Channel Five party and I think at the very beginning it was definitely very touch and go as to what cheek he choose — either the left cheek or the right cheek. And when one Cheeky did respond, Lembit got in there!

VANESSA FELTZ on Lembit Öpik

Cherie Blair's just brought out her autobiography hasn't she? If Gordon Brown's wife did the same it'd probably be less eventful than Anne Frank's. Monday, stayed in, Gordon cried.

FRANKIE BOYLE

William Hague, the world's favourite hairline.

RORY BREMNER

If you travel to the States they have a lot of different words than like what we use. For instance: they say "elevator", we say "lift"; they say "drapes", we say "curtains"; they say "president", we say "seriously deranged git".

ALEXEI SAYLE on George W Bush

Jordan, that attractive young woman with the frightening breasts, stood for election in Manchester in 2001 and polled just 713 votes. You would bonk Jordan but you certainly wouldn't vote for her. That's the British view and it seems to me an eminently sensible one.

ROD LIDDLE

The one good thing about global warming is that as the waters rise, Hazel Blears will drown first.

ANONYMOUS LABOUR MP, about the pint-sized ex-cabinet minister

Americans only re-elected George Bush to prove they had a sense of irony.

SCOTT CAPURRO

At one moment Portillo was polishing his jackboots and planning the advance. Next thing he shows up as a TV presenter. It is rather like Pol Pot joining the *Teletubbies*.

TONY BANKS on Michael Portillo

Shoulders like Frank Bruno and bears an undeniable resemblance to an only slightly effeminate Geordie trucker.

LYNDA LEE-POTTER on Mo Mowlam

Cherie's bottom is too wide, her thighs too podgy, her ankles too thick....

LYNDA LEE-POTTER on Cherie Blair

Everybody loves Bill. Bill is adorable and Bill is always flattering me and inviting me to stuff in Britain and we're buddy-buddy, and I like him. I don't like Hillary because she's so bossy and cold and manipulative and stuff.

GERMAINE GREER on Bill and Hillary Clinton

Don't give me all that crap about the feminist vote,
she's fucking hopeless. If she's honest she should
campaign on the "I'm fucking useless" vote.

ALAN MILBURN on Harriet Harman

You know what we've got? We've got trash in the White
House. Trash is a thing that is colourblind, it can cross
all eco-socionomic categories.

TAMMY BRUCE on Barack and Michelle Obama

Tony Blair is only Bill Clinton with his zip done up.

NEIL HAMILTON

Just heard in the news that in ten years' time there'll
be more pensioners than young people. What a
terrifying statistic, for the country's paedophiles. No
wonder Gary Glitter didn't want to come back.

FRANKIE BOYLE

He's not too keen on women. I don't think he's too keen
on very much. He should kick off his red socks and
settle down with a nice brandy and a porn film.
PETER O'TOOLE on Pope Benedict XVI

Christopher… didn't care if the Red Army
watered its horses at Hendon.
**PETER HITCHENS on brother Christopher Hitchens, sparking
a four-year feud**

Tony Blair has as much charisma as a pair of dentures
grinning in a glass of water.
TREVOR BAYLISS

It must be the single most successful emotional con
job of the twentieth century.
CHRISTOPHER HITCHENS on Mother Teresa

All black with an eye-burning red panel that splattered itself down the front like a geometrical haemorrhage.

GERMAINE GREER on the dress that Michelle Obama wore to her husband's US election declaration

There is something of the night about him.

ANN WIDDECOMBE on Michael Howard

He is racist, he's homophobic, he's xenophobic and he's a sexist. He's the perfect Republican candidate.

BILL PRESS on Pat Buchanan

The culture of blackshirt and brownshirt pseudomasculinity, as has often been pointed out, depended on some keen shared interests. Among them were massively repressed homoerotic fantasies, a camp interest in military uniforms, an obsession with flogging and a hatred of silky and effeminate Jews. Well, I mean to say, have you seen Mel's movie?

CHRISTOPHER HITCHENS on *The Passion of The Christ*

Dan Quayle is more stupid than Ronald Reagan
put together.

MATT GROENING

Can you bloody imagine it? He'd be scary. He would
roar around London in a Lamborghini with a huge
mayoral flagpole, shooting cyclists.

RICHARD HAMMOND on Jeremy Clarkson as Mayor of London

He may be a liar, but at least he's the people's liar.

ANDY HAMILTON on Tony Blair

Instead of his "what you see is what you get" slogan, a
better catchphrase would be "I'm not quite as
creepy as I come across".

ANDY HAMILTON on Michael Howard

A lager lout.

MICHAEL HESELTINE on John Prescott

Bush seems to fill every job in his cabinet with some incompetent Jesus freak, and it seems to me tremendously hypocritical to fill the one job that he really cares about, the guy who gets him elected, with an atheist.

BILL MAHER on Karl Rove

I have a big dossier of his past, and I did not even have to sex it up.

MICHAEL HOWARD on Tony Blair

My lies are silk while his are made of polyester.

ALAN JOHNSON on Gordon Brown

Today was Arnold Schwarzenegger's inauguration as Governor of California. Arnold was told to "Raise your right hand and butcher the English language after me".

CRAIG KILBORN

YouTube if you want to...

HAZEL BLEARS attacking Gordon Brown's appearance on YouTube

Brown is a little tiny dot in this world.

ROBERT MUGABE on Gordon Brown

The House has noticed the Prime Minister's remarkable transformation in the last few weeks from Stalin to Mr Bean. Creating chaos out of order rather than order out of chaos.

VINCE CABLE on Gordon Brown

An analogue prime minister in a digital age.

DAVID CAMERON on Gordon Brown

He might as well have a corncob up his arse.

ALAN CLARK on Douglas Hurd

She probably thinks Sinai is the plural of sinus.

JONATHAN AITKEN on Margaret Thatcher

I hate Michael Sheen as Tony. Doesn't do it for me at all. Tony is six foot and quite broad-shouldered and Michael isn't six foot and isn't strapping and doesn't have that physical presence.

CHERIE BLAIR

Bill Clinton is a man who thinks international affairs mean dating a girl from out of town.

TOM CLANCY

The Dalai Lama visited the White House and told the President that he could teach him to find a higher state of consciousness. Then after talking to Bush for a few minutes, he said, "You know what? Let's just grab lunch".

BILL MAHER

He is like a bad comic working the crowd. A moron, if you'll pardon the expression.

MARTIN SHEEN on George W Bush

In England the Queen is the head of the church as well as head of the state — you have to pay for both. When she dies her slobbering, weak-chinned Dauphin of a son will be the head of the Church of England, and he wants to convert to Islam in the meantime. And that is what you get when you found a church on the family values of Henry VIII.

CHRISTOPHER HITCHENS

It's like being savaged by a dead sheep.

DENIS HEALEY on being attacked by Geoffrey Howe

Really, very nice voice, and the voice of a very thoughtful person who… you could say had matured… you get the feeling he will keep on growing… you don't get that feeling about her, you get the feeling that she's shrivelling, if you follow me closely here.

CHRISTOPHER HITCHENS on the relative endowment of Barack Obama and Hillary Clinton

Peter Mandelson is someone who can skulk in broad daylight.

SIMON HOGGART

When she speaks without thinking, she says what she thinks.

LORD ST JOHN OF FAWSLEY on Margaret Thatcher

Margaret Thatcher in drag.

Former-New Zealand Prime Minister DAVID LANGE on Tony Blair

On TV he turns into one of the Thunderbirds, speaking in a relentless monotone, performing one of the worst stage smirks I've ever seen when he thinks he should lighten up a bit.

PIERS MORGAN on Gordon Brown

He appears to have no clear political view except that the world should be a nicer place and that he should be loved and trusted by everyone and questioned by no one.

NORMAN TEBBIT on Tony Blair

The Clinton White House today said they would start to give national security and intelligence briefings to George Bush. I don't know how well this is working out. Today after the first one Bush said, "I've got one question: What colour is the red phone?"

BILL MAHER

David Cameron plays by far the most convincing Blair. The rest of us just do the voice and the mannerisms, but Cameron does the whole career.

RORY BREMNER

U2 lead singer Bono met with President Bush at the White House. Bono urged the President to help the world's poor. Bush urged Bono to get back with Cher.

TINA FEY

California governor Arnold Schwarzenegger's popularity has been slipping in recent months as residents slowly begin to realize they elected Arnold Schwarzenegger to be their governor.

TINA FEY

David Cameron is no different from Tony Blair. He's like a songwriter who's eternally ripping off someone else's song and just changing the odd line a little.

NOEL GALLAGHER

I confess, it was pretty riveting when John McCain trotted out Sarah Palin for the first time. Like many people, I thought, "Damn, a hyperconservative, fuckable, Type A, antiabortion, Christian Stepford wife in a 'sexy librarian' costume – as a vice president? That's a brilliant stroke of horrifyingly cynical pandering to the Christian right".

CINTRA WILSON

The trouble with Michael Heseltine is that he has had to buy all his furniture.

ALAN CLARK

Bad Mother Palin is blabbing about how her pregnant teenage daughter has made the right CHOICE!!! Well, first of all......your slutty daughter wouldn't have a CHOICE to make at all, if you had your way... I can see that she gets off talking badly to Barack, and I am sure the "N" word is rollin' around that empty head of hers somewhere.

ROSEANNE BARR on Sarah Palin

It's like a really bad Disney movie... it's a really terrifying possibility... I need to know if she really thinks that dinosaurs were here 4,000 years ago. I want to know that, I really do. Because she's gonna' have the nuclear codes.

MATT DAMON on Sarah Palin

Al Sharpton — I refuse to call him Reverend — anyway I don't think Reverend is a title of honour. He's a Pentecostalist so called. I've never heard him speak in tongues, though I have heard him babble a lot.

CHRISTOPHER HITCHENS on Alfred Charles Sharpton, Jr.

Her greatest hypocrisy is in her pretence that she is a woman.

WENDY DONIGER on Sarah Palin

I mean, let's face it, we didn't have slavery in this country for over 100 years because it was a bad thing. Quite the opposite: slavery built the South. I'm not saying we should bring it back; I'm just saying it had its merits. For one thing, the streets were safer after dark.

RUSH LIMBAUGH

He is your typical smiling, brilliant, back-stabbing, bullshitting southern nut-cutter.

LANE KIRKLAND on Jimmy Carter

Jim Bakker spells his name with two K's because three would be too obvious.

BILL MAHER

I suppose it means that if I did run for office, no one could say I was the worst actor ever to be elected.

BEN AFFLECK on Arnold Schwarzenegger

A senescent bimbo with a lust for home furnishings.

BARBARA EHRENREICH on Nancy Reagan

See, Barack been, um, talking down to black people on this faith based – I wanna' cut his nuts off.

REV. JESSE JACKSON on Barack Obama

You can't be nine religions in three years.

SHERROD SMALL on Madonna

I'm scared for the world. This guy is obviously an idiot. He can't speak… I'd do a better job than him – and I'm not very bright!

ROBBIE WILLIAMS on George W Bush

You know who deserves a posthumous Medal of
Honour? James Earl Ray. We miss you,
James. Godspeed.

RUSH LIMBAUGH

If Britons were left to tax themselves, there would be no
schools, no hospitals, just a 500-mile-high statue of
Diana, Princess of Wales.

ANDY ZALTZMAN

If we were a band of survivors do you think we'd elect
Gordon Brown to lead us? He'd be like the village idiot.
And if David Cameron hadn't gone to Eton? He'd be
managing a Pizza Hut. The minute I get cancer I'm
killing all of Britain's politicians.

FRANKIE BOYLE

No one grows up wanting to be a junkie, eat Utterly
Butterly or listen to Phil Collins – capitalism
wears you down.

JEREMY HARDY

When a woman reaches orgasm with a man she is only collaborating with the patriarchal system, eroticizing her own oppression.

SHEILA JEFFRYS

. . . drink-sodden former Trotskyist popinjay.

GEORGE GALLOWAY on Christopher Hitchens

Heterosexual intercourse is the pure, formalized expression of contempt for women's bodies.

ANDREA DWORKIN

He struck me as the type who would stand at the back of the dance hall and move his shoulders.

Britain's Got Talent **winner GEORGE SAMPSON on David Cameron**

Compared to the Clintons, Reagan is living proof that a Republican with half a brain is better than a Democrat with two.

P. J. O'ROURKE

I'd like to throw eggs at Tony Blair just once before he goes. Not that it would make a dent — nothing bloody seems to.

ZANDRA RHODES

Too full of drugs, obesity, underachievement and Labour MPs.

BORIS JOHNSON on Portsmouth

He has spent all that money on his smile, but he won't even throw us one. He won't win over Kylie like that.

DAVID CAMERON on Gordon Brown

Have you ever noticed how all composite pictures of wanted criminals resemble Jesse Jackson?

RUSH LIMBAUGH

I am going to hang Saakashvili by the balls.

VLADIMIR PUTIN on Georgia's president

If life were fair, Dan Quayle would be making a living asking, "Do you want fries with that?"

JOHN CLEESE

He's a perfectly charming person who would water your roses while you were on holiday, but as leader of the main campaigning body against racism in Britain he's been a complete dud.

KEN LIVINGSTONE on Trevor Phillips

If I had an hour to live, I'd like to listen to one of Gordon Brown's pre-budget statements. It's not that I find them exciting and uplifting, but if I only had an hour to live, I'd like it to seem as long as possible.

DR EAMONN BUTLER

You strike me as a very boring man. Are you a boring man?

IAN LIDDELL-GRAINGER to Sir Christopher Kelly

Bill Clinton's foreign policy experience is pretty much confined to having had breakfast once at the International House of Pancakes.

PAT BUCHANAN

A sweet national joke with funny ears, who looks like a womble.

DAVID STARKEY on Dr Rowan Williams

Those who sleep with dogs will get fleas.

NORMAN TEBBIT on George Osborne

He doesn't dye his hair – he's just prematurely orange.

GERALD FORD on Ronald Reagan

Why should I have that guy running down the country? Who the fuck is he?

PETER MANDELSON on Starbucks owner Howard Schultz

A lot of people are scared of him, not just because of his position but because of his temper. I don't think he ever had time for la dolce vita.

CARLA BRUNI on her husband Nicolas Sarkozy

He is like some sherry-crazed old dowager who has lost the family silver at roulette, and who now decides to double up by betting the house as well.

BORIS JOHNSON on Gordon Brown

He's the biggest celebrity in the world.
But is he ready to lead?

JOHN McCAIN on Barack Obama

The Goebbels of Scientology.

THOMAS GANDOW, spokesman on religious cults, on Tom Cruise

How did Bush go from being an alcoholic bum to the most powerful figure in the world?

OLIVER STONE

In a series of TV interviews this morning, Hillary Clinton said her favourite movie as a little girl was *The Wizard of Oz*. Her favourite movie in college was *Casablanca*. Then, after she got married it was *Kill Bill*.

JAY LENO

Clinton lied. A man might forget where he parks or where he lives, but he never forgets oral sex, no matter how bad it is.

BARBARA BUSH

If David Cameron puts his hand out to youth, he's going to get it bitten off.

GOLDIE

I don't want my picture taken with a war criminal.

PAUL WELLER on Tony Blair

I was going to have a few comments about John Edwards but you have to go into rehab if you use the word faggot.

ANN COULTER

I mean, you got the first mainstream African-American who is articulate and bright and clean and a nice-looking guy, I mean, that's a storybook, man.

JOE BIDEN on Barack Obama

Go fuck yourself.

Vice President DICK CHENEY to Senator Patrick Leahy on the Senate floor

Christ would not vote for Barack Obama, because Barack Obama has voted to behave in a way that it is inconceivable for Christ to have behaved.

ALAN KEYES

He's too snore-y and stinky, they don't want to
ever get into bed with him.

**MICHELLE OBAMA on her daughters' refusal to crawl into bed in
the morning with her husband Barack**

I think it's a pity there isn't a hell for him to go to.

CHRISTOPHER HITCHENS on Reverend Jerry Falwell

She is a monster, too – that is off the record – she is
stooping to anything.

Obama aide SAMANTHA POWERS on Hillary Clinton

This is a stain on his legacy, much worse, much deeper,
than the one on Monica's blue dress.

**Obama adviser GORDON FISCHER, on Bill Clinton's
attacks on Obama**

If John Kerry had a dollar for every time he bragged
about serving in Vietnam – oh wait, he does.

ANN COULTER

Fucking Jews… The Jews are responsible for all the wars in the world… Are you a Jew?

MEL GIBSON to Malibu police after being arrested for drunk driving

How could you have stayed eight years with a man who has such ridiculous calves?

NICOLAS SARKOZY to Carla Bruni on her ex Mick Jagger

Cheney's defence is that he was aiming at a quail when he shot the guy. Which means that Cheney now has the worst aim of anyone in the White House since Bill Clinton.

JAY LENO

President Obama and his lovely wife, Michelle, recently went out to dinner at a restaurant. And after dinner, they took a romantic sunset walk around the White House grounds. And I was thinking, well, Bill Clinton used to take romantic strolls, but I think he waited until his wife was out of town.

DAVID LETTERMAN

David Cameron's body is good but his face is all wrong.
He could do with some blond highlights and a spray
tan. He's far too pasty.

PARIS HILTON

I'm not going to get into a name-calling match with
somebody who has a nine percent approval rating.

HARRY REID on Dick Cheney

. . . semi-house-trained polecat.

MICHAEL FOOT on Norman Tebbit

It's the sort of thing parents might chant encouragingly
to a child slow on the potty-training.

CHRISTOPHER HITCHENS on Barack Obama's slogan "Yes, We Can"

. . . [has] the sensitivity of a sex-starved
boa-constrictor.

TONY BANKS on Margaret Thatcher

Living proof that a pig's bladder on the end of a stick can be elected to Parliament.

TONY BANKS on Terry Dicks

She is a bounder, a liar, a deceiver, a cheat and a crook.

TAM DALYELL on Margaret Thatcher

. . . mostly hideous — they have no fragrance and I dislike women who deny their femininity. They are just cagmags, scrub heaps, old tattles.

SIR NICHOLAS FAIRBAIRN on women MPs

Mr Blair is responsible for inflicting on Britain its most grievous foreign policy disaster since Suez. Among his own people, who would hire him to mow the grass?

MAX HASTINGS on Tony Blair

Alastair Campbell — scowling, surly, crew-cut — has become the unacceptable face of New Labour.

ROBERT HARRIS

The problem with the French is that they don't have a word for entrepreneur.

GEORGE W BUSH

He's a political iPod. Tories can download the policy they want.

RORY BREMNER on David Cameron

If Sarah Palin becomes Vice President, will she be shortchanging her kids or will she be shortchanging the country?

AMY ROBACH

I have a great deal of difficulty with the idea of the ideal man. As far as I'm concerned, men are the product of a damaged gene. They pretend to be normal but what they're doing sitting there with benign smiles on their faces is they're manufacturing sperm. They do it all the time. They never stop.

GERMAINE GREER on men

PRESENTERS
&
CHATSHOWS

I'm worth a thousand BBC journalists.

JONATHAN ROSS

I would particularly like to thank Jonathan and Russell
who have made me famous. You're great guys,
I love you.

ANDREW SACHS accepting the Oldie of the Year award.

What I did is the same as millions of men before me.
I'm not a Gary Glitter and there are no dead people at
the bottom of my swimming pool.

CHRIS TARRANT on his divorce

We'll beat him when he pops his clogs.

CHRIS MOYLES on Terry Wogan

Change gear, change gear, change gear, check mirror,
murder a prostitute, change gear, change gear, murder.
That's a lot of effort in a day.

JEREMY CLARKSON on lorry drivers

I have the feeling about sixty percent of what you say is crap.

DAVID LETTERMAN, to FOX News' Bill O'Reilly

You have the charisma of a damp flannel... You're better off rearing your goats back in Yorkshire, love.

JANET STREET-PORTER to Selina Scott

Vernon Kay is as edgy as cottage cheese.

MIRANDA SAWYER

Don't you think that Davina McCall, who shrieks like a fire alarm through a mouth as big as a train tunnel, is just the epitome of feminine grace?

JOE JOSEPH

Piers Morgan... is sculpted from lard.

JONATHAN ROSS

I am seriously enjoying my latest spat with Jonathan Ross. I reckon it would be easy to beat him in a punch-up and I can't wait!

PIERS MORGAN

Anthea, how about we get together while I kick you in the mouth?

CHRIS EVANS on Anthea Turner

But this recession is affecting everyone, even celebrities. Victoria Beckham hasn't eaten for three weeks. Charlie Sheen has been forced to have sex without paying for it. It's true. And even Madonna has had to get rid of one of her personal assistants: our thoughts go out to you Guy Ritchie.

SACHA BARON COHEN at The Golden Globes 2009

She couldn't edit a bus ticket.

KELVIN MACKENZIE on Janet Street-Porter

I've always been a staunch defender of a woman's right to make-up, but there's more pancake on that poor woman's face than at a Shrove Tuesday cook-in. And as for the hair! Keeping that hydraulic assembly aloft must take enough Elnett to blow a hole the size of Siberia in the ozone layer.

AMANDA PLATELL on Natasha Kaplinsky

Watching *The One Show* with Adrian Chiles: it's like being trapped in the buffet car of a slow-moving express train with a toby jug that's somehow learned to speak; a speaking toby jug filled to the brim with piss… it makes me long for the days when a regional accent was considered a professional disadvantage.

STEWART LEE on Adrian Chiles

Do you mind if I sit back a little? Because your breath is very bad.

DONALD TRUMP to Larry King

As talentless and unattractive as Jade Goody.

ROD LIDDLE on Piers Morgan

Tess Daly is a good example of the young crowd of presenters who are pretty useless.

ULRIKA JONSSON

I have tried to analyse just what it is about Fiona Bruce that makes me hit the off button before she utters a single word. Is it her flirtatious, conspiratorial smile? Her habit of stressing the wrong words in every sentence? The exaggeratedly slow bedtime-story tone that prevents any headline from sounding more serious than a broken nail?

PHILIP NORMAN

Like Anne Robinson in a Korean restaurant, it'll be dog eat dog.

GRAHAM NORTON

Morgan shows himself to be an ill-mannered, thin-skinned, easily flattered, narcissistic ignoramus, given to stupid jokes, banal observations, casual rudeness and hypocritical pieties.

DAVID AARONOVITCH on Piers Morgan

By the year 2015 all newspaper articles will be delivered to your cerebral cortex via wireless connection the moment they're written. Apart from Richard Littlejohn's columns, because he won't be writing them any more. Instead he'll scrape a living masturbating for pennies in abandoned shop doorways.

CHARLIE BROOKER

Des O'Connor is suffering from a hernia. Is it any wonder? He's been carrying Melanie Sykes for years.

GARRY BUSHELL

Evans is caught in some Eighties time warp, as dated
as a Sony Walkman in an iPod world.

AMANDA PLATELL on Chris Evans

Kim and Aggie: cleaners who became celebrities. Like
the Cheeky Girls in reverse.

JONATHAN ROSS

He fucked your granddaughter... I'm sorry I apologise.
Andrew, I apologise, I got excited, what can I say
– it just came out.

**JONATHAN ROSS leaving a message on Andrew Sachs's
answer phone**

She was bent over the couch...

**JONATHAN ROSS leaving a message on Andrew Sachs's
answer phone**

I said some things I didn't of oughta', like I had sex with your granddaughter. But it was consensual and she wasn't menstrual, it was consensual lovely sex.

RUSSELL BRAND leaving a message on Andrew Sachs's answer phone

What a hypocrite he is and what a shabby man he has turned out to be. Shame on him.

GEORGINA BAILLIE on Jonathan Ross

I will only say he's a disappointment in the bedroom considering he has had so much practice.

GEORGINA BAILLIE on Russell Brand

There is nothing decent about Russell Brand – he's a despicable rat.

GEORGINA BAILLIE

He's just a sex-obsessed ex-junkie, a pre-Raphaelite version of Bernard Manning who will say literally anything to make a cheap tabloid headline, however lewd, crude or downright disgusting.

PIERS MORGAN on Russell Brand

Ross always professes to be so protective about his own family. Though in reality, he's just a shameless hypocrite like so many other celebrities.

PIERS MORGAN on Jonathan Ross

I just think that this man is like sort of one of those, you know, snake-oil salesmen in *Little House on the Prairie*.

ROSIE O'DONNELL on Donald Trump

Rosie will rue the words she said. I'll most likely sue her for making those false statements — and it'll be fun. Rosie's a loser. A real loser. I look forward to making tons of money from my nice fat little Rosie.

DONALD TRUMP on Rosie O'Donnell

Rosie O'Donnell's disgusting, I mean both inside and out. You take a look at her, she's a slob, she talks like a truck driver… she's basically a disaster.

DONALD TRUMP on Rosie O'Donnell

Rosie's a person that's very lucky to have her girlfriend and she'd better be careful or I'll send one of my friends over to pick up her girlfriend; why would she stay with Rosie if she had another choice?

DONALD TRUMP on Rosie O'Donnell

Oprah, Uma; Uma, Oprah…

**A lame joke by DAVID LETTERMAN at the 1995 Academy Awards
which allegedly sparked a feud between the two talk show hosts**

Nice to be patronised by a man who's bought so much
quality to the world of television.

PAUL MERTON to Jerry Springer

It is not really possible to present a satirical
programme if you are seen to be sleazier than the
people you are making jokes about. You do not have to
occupy much of the moral high ground to do this job.
But you do need a few inches.

IAN HISLOP on Angus Deayton

The Welsh… I mean, what are they for?

ANNE ROBINSON

REALITY TV

I watched *Celebrity Love Island* because Jonathan Ross said that Abi Titmuss and Rebecca Loos were crying. But when I turned it on they were having a good time so I turned it off... Think if the rest of the world got wiped out and humanity had to start again with that lot. You'd be left with a bunch of ropey old sluts and desperate wannabees.

RICKY GERVAIS

I do believe that his world is about to come crashing down around him very soon. At least I hope so, I hate him.

RIK WALLER on Simon Cowell

Fuck off home.

DANIELLE LLOYD to Shilpa Shetty on *Celebrity Big Brother*

Go back to the slums.

JADE GOODY to Shilpa Shetty on *Celebrity Big Brother*

Simon Cowell... buffed to the sheen of an ornamental pebble.

TANYA GOLD

Who's judging *American Idol*? Paula Abdul? Paula Abdul judging a singing contest is like Christopher Reeve judging a dance contest!

CHRIS ROCK

Jade Goody is part woman and part scientific blunder.

JEREMY CLARKSON

Expecting Jade Goody to take any place in a civilised society is akin to employing a monkey as a butler.

FRANKIE BOYLE

Tonight's the final of *X-Factor*, and there's *Strictly Come Dancing* too. And you know what? I'd rather have my cock bitten off by an Alsatian than watch either.

ELTON JOHN

You're a liar and a fake. You're not in Neverland here, you're not no Princess, you are normal so learn to live with it. You need a day in the slums......What's her surname anyway? Shilpa Cookamada? Shilpa Rockamada? Is it Shilpa Poppadom?

JADE GOODY, *Celebrity Big Brother*

. . . too orange to be taken seriously.

KATIE HOPKINS on fellow *The Apprentice* contestant,
Kristina Grimes

. . . just happy to be out of the underwear factory for the day.

KATIE HOPKINS on fellow *The Apprentice* contestant Michelle Mone

Seeing Scott Henshaw refuse to eat an anus was like
watching Red Rum pull up at Beecher's Brook.

JIMMY CARR on *I'm a Celebrity Get Me Out of Here*

Alan Sugar shrieks like a huge indignant hedgehog at
the point of climax.

CHARLIE BROOKER

She's no wonder girl. How many times has she had sex?
Probably very few and not very often… These girls are
very precious. Their bodies are so special that no man
may penetrate it. She is difficult.

JOHN McCRIRICK on Shilpa Shetty

If I am feeling mean and I know that she's feeling
sensitive, then I can't help myself.

SIMON COWELL on Paula Abdul

A woman with improbably raised eyebrows and snail trails of Botox over her perfectly smooth face… flat-packed, hair-ironed, over-plucked monstrous fool.

TANYA GOLD on Amanda Holden

Who wants to watch her wailing in self-pity about her druggie past? Not me, thanks very much.

JORDAN on Sophie Anderton's appearance on
I'm a Celebrity Get Me Out of Here

I can't believe she's being paid for interviews on subjects that people are really traumatised by.

JORDAN after Jade Goody went public about her cancer

Jade Goody: men all over the country want to take her home and shag her brains in.

JONATHAN ROSS

I welcome him like I welcome cold sores.

PAULA ABDUL on Simon Cowell

Paula's a pain in the ass. She's just one of those irritating people. I keep my time with her to a minimum.

SIMON COWELL on Paula Abdul

Can you imagine Simon as a kid? His imaginary friends probably never wanted to play with him.

PAULA ABDUL on Simon Cowell

Jade Goody's the only woman I can think of who always makes the rest of us feel slim, fit and talented.

AMANDA PLATELL

It was like someone trying to move a fridge. It was like she's never learned to walk.

JONATHAN ROSS on Fiona Phillips on *Strictly Come Dancing*

On the face of it the wedding of Jade Goody and Jack
Tweed was every single little thing every right-thinking
man and woman in this country has come to loathe —
the very recrudescence of the canker that infests
the social body.

WILL SELF

You know what Rik Waller's body fat was? Sixty percent.
I looked that up. That is the same percent as
a pork scratching.

RICKY GERVAIS

She is only famous for managing a brain-dead
rock star.

**Model and reality gameshow contestant MEGAN HAUSERMAN on
Sharon Osbourne, whose reaction allegedly led to her becoming a
suspect in a case of minor battery**

When we clear the media smoke screen from around her death what we're left with is a woman who came to represent all that's paltry and wretched about Britain today.

MICHAEL PARKINSON on Jade Goody

John Sergeant's sturdy performance highlights one of life's great truths that ugly men do remarkably well with the ladies.

ESTHER RANTZEN

It's about time you started taking responsibility for your failed version of *The Apprentice*. Your performance was terrible in that the show lacked mood, temperament and just about everything else a show needs for success. I knew it would fail as soon as I first saw it — and your low ratings bore me out.

DONALD TRUMP in an open letter to Martha Stewart

When Preston was touring with Paul Weller he had credibility with his band; now that he's trying to stay famous by pretending to be in love with Chantelle, he's lost all credibility and the only fans he has now are young girls who don't know anything about real music.

JODIE MARSH on Samuel Preston

I'm not bitter. I'm stating what I think, which is that she's a waste of space, she's talentless and that if she hadn't married Preston, no one would give a flying fuck about either of them. The minute they get divorced, she'll be finished.

JODIE MARSH on Samuel Preston and Chantelle Houghton

A man so slow he probably has to whistle before he goes to the toilet so he knows which end to shit through.

CHARLIE BROOKER on Jack Tweed

ROCK & POP

Amidst this haze of sex, drugs and rock and roll, Amy Wineglass has just been released on bail.

JON SNOW

Sleeping with George Michael would be like having sex with a groundhog.

BOY GEORGE

I would have thought you'd actually have to be able to remember your life to write about it.

MICK JAGGER on Keith Richards

I don't think adopting a child is a good idea given your lifestyle. I think you'd be better off adopting a highway mile.

GREG FITZSIMMONS to Jessica Simpson

She got rid of all her piercings except the nipple ring. Why? Because the nipple ring is classy.

MICHAEL COLTON on Christina Aguilera

What is the difference between God and Bono? God doesn't wander down Grafton Street thinking he's Bono.
LOUIS WALSH

It's like getting a Louis Vuitton handbag… she bought a baby, for God's sake.
SHARON OSBOURNE on Madonna's adoption of David Banda

Those vile veiny hands, that sad stringy neck – yuck! Liz MacDonald off Corrie looks ten times better.
JULIE BURCHILL on Madonna

I can't believe Amy Winehouse self-harms. She's so irritating she must be able to find someone to do it for her.
ZOE LYONS

50 Cent, or as he's called over here, approximately 29p.

SARAH KENDALL

I believe in my heart that if Jesus were alive today he would be doing the same thing.

MADONNA, defending the crucifixion scene in her Confessions tour

Dump her friends… fire the stylist. Be sensible. Put her in rehearsal for four weeks; get her into the gym [because] when she's on it, she's incredible.

SIMON COWELL on Britney Spears

I'm not old enough to know a lot of them but even I know that Take That were bollocks.

ALEX TURNER at Q Awards

I guess I really should thank our kid for singing all these great songs – but as he's not here, fuck him.

NOEL GALLAGHER on brother Liam at Q Awards

I find it a bit creepy if you're having sex with people the same age as your children.

JERRY HALL on Mick Jagger

P. Diddy… would like to be the next James Bond. In fact, he's already changed his name again to "Double-O-Diddy".

DAVID LETTERMAN

Like Madonna and Prince, you know you've made it in pop when you can go by one name – it's Sophie Ellis-Bextor.

SIMON ANSTELL

I was asked to produce Craig David. I couldn't believe it. I was mildly insulted and a bit gutted, frankly.

IAN PARTON

I keep hearing about mutha fucking Harry Potter. Who is this muthafucker?

SNOOP DOGG

What a vain, preening little shit he is! Was that the hardest bit of doing a Blue video? Acting like Duncan wasn't a terrible shit?

SIMON AMSTELL to Lee Ryan on former colleague Duncan James

When it comes to couture chaos, this tacky terror should take a bow — looks like an over-the-hill Lolita. From the princess of pop to the ultimate fashion flop.

MR BLACKWELL on Britney Spears

He's from England, he's angry and he's got Mad Power Disease.

PAULA ABDUL on Simon Cowell

I don't remember where I was but I was really pleased he was dead, as he was a wife-beater, gay-basher, anti-Semite and all-round bully-boy.

JULIE BURCHILL on the assassination of John Lennon

It would be true to say that two of them are really ugly.

SIMON COWELL on N Sync

Visions of that greasy muff, which one could easily have fried an egg on without benefit of oil, haunt me till this very day.

JULIE BURCHILL on Madonna's book *SEX*

It seems to me that when you reach the kind of acclaim that she's reached… you should be a little more magnanimous and a little less of a c**t.

CHER on Madonna

I could take off all my clothes and stand on the freeway, but would that make me an artist?

JANET JACKSON on Madonna's book *SEX*

He sings like he's throwing up.

ANDREW O'CONNOR on Bryan Ferry

Chris Martin looks like a geography teacher. What's all that with writing messages about Free Trade on his hand when he's playing. If he wants to write things down I'll give him a pen and a pad of paper. Bunch of students.

LIAM GALLAGHER

Presley sounded like Jayne Mansfield looked – blowsy and loud and low.

JULIE BURCHILL

Someone has got to tell the Rolling Stones that they are no longer sexually attractive men, 'cos they look like cigarette butts with bad hair.

DAVID BADDIEL

He's an arsehole and I think every gay person with a brain cell found it hideously offensive to see Elton performing with him. It's like me singing with Pol Pot.

BOY GEORGE on Eminem and Elton John

Ronnie Wood looks like a blow-dried crow.

SEAN LOCK

Kenny Everett-in-waiting, because Kenny Everett's dead
and it's only a matter of time before
John pops his clogs.

CHRIS MOYLES on John Peel

If your son asks for a Hannah Montana MP3 player, you
might want to already think about putting him down
for adoption before he brings his
… erm… partner home.

JONATHAN ROSS

He and David think they are the King and Queen of
England and can tell everyone what to do.

RUPERT EVERETT on Elton John and David Furnish

The Beatles were peripheral. If you had more knowledge
about music, it didn't really mean anything.

VAN MORRISON

There is always a member who thinks he's black.
Boyzone's Shane always does a sort of menacing "I'm
hip" face. I find it very amusing.

ROBBIE WILLIAMS on boy bands

It's a friendly feud but it's not possible for Kanye to beat me. It's the teddy bear versus the gorilla. Kanye sucks.

50 CENT on Kanye West

I hate that Alex and Damon. I hope they catch AIDS and die.

NOEL GALLAGHER on Alex James and Damon Albarn

I just think it was a shame when they started appearing in *Hello* and *OK* magazines. For me that just seemed such a betrayal of what they were all about. So I don't know where do you go from there?

DAMON ALBARN on Liam and Noel Gallagher

J-Lo as your step mother. Excellent. Before you're even old enough to say ,"You're not my real mom" she's married to someone else.

PAUL F. TOMPKINS

It's like three-year-olds' music worse than Steps.
LIAM GALLAGHER on Gorillaz

. . . fucking drama queen.
LIAM GALLAGHER on Robbie Williams' rehab

Dizzee Rascal is a bit much for me. He sounds like a twelve-year-old boy on the brink of puberty.
CHARLOTTE CHURCH

So, anybody like to see me fight Liam? Would you pay to come and see it? Liam, a hundred grand of your money and a hundred grand of my money. We'll get in a ring and we'll have a fight and you can all watch it on TV.
ROBBIE WILLIAMS to Liam Gallagher at the BRITs

[I'll] lead her through the forest of her sexuality.
CHRIS MOYLES offering to take the virginity of Charlotte Church when she turned 16

Marilyn Manson: made entirely from Cher offcuts.

MARK LAMARR

The Kooks sound like they're rolling over and begging Radio One to fuck them.

JOHNNY BORRELL

. . . greedy prima donna.

DAVE GROHL on Courtney Love

Dave gets to walk away unscathed and be the happy guy in rock, when he's one of the biggest jerks.

COURTNEY LOVE on Dave Grohl

Gary Barlow's walking like he needs a poo.

CHRIS MOYLES on the Comic Relief Mount Kilimanjaro climb

. . . peroxide drenched homophobic has-been.

NICK CANNON on Eminem

I already did that [peed on her].

EMINEM on Mariah Carey

What shall we call our son so he does not get the shit kicked out of him at school? We shall call him Englebert Humperdink! Yes, that'll work.

EDDIE IZZARD

I'm sick of her because I have no respect for the way she utilizes her talent. She could do so many things that are more constructive.

JENNIFER JASON LEIGH on Madonna

Another kid already?

SEAN PENN to Madonna on her 21-year-old Brazilian lover,

Jesus Luz

Over my dead body. She needs to stop doing drugs and get a grip. Then maybe we'll talk.

**STEVIE NICKS on rumours that Lindsay Lohan
wants to play her on film**

That witch tricked me into spreading lies about Paul… At one stage we were so close I viewed her as the daughter I never had. Today I think of her as the witch I wish I never met.

Former PR manager MICHELE ELYZABETH on Heather Mills

You're crap!

**BRIAN McFADDEN at the Brit Awards sparking a feud with
So Solid Crew**

It's just unfortunate that Moby wasn't injured. My drummer has offered to beat him up with one arm.

MARILYN MANSON

Madonna is only fifty but she's got the body of a man half her age.

JIMMY CARR

This song is for the emotionally retarded. Maybe you know some people who fall into that category.

MADONNA on Guy Ritchie

. . . the ropey-looking ginger one at the back.

CHRIS MOYLES on Nicola Roberts of Girls Aloud

Like cuddling up to a piece of grissle.

GUY RITCHIE on Madonna

I don't want to look like Cheryl Tweedy! It's tongue in cheek, it's meant to be ironic.

LILY ALLEN on the lyrics to her number 1 single, Smile

. . . chick with a dick.

CHERYL COLE on Lily Allen

Cheryl, if you're reading this, I may not be as pretty as you, but at least I write and sing my own songs without the aid of Auto-Tune. I must say, taking your clothes off, doing sexy dancing and marrying a rich footballer must be very gratifying, your mother must be so proud, stupid bitch.

LILY ALLEN on Cheryl Cole

Charlotte's a nasty little piece of work with a fat head. Her publicity stunts slagging everyone off haven't worked. I don't know who she and her scabby boyfriend think they are.

CHERYL COLE on Charlotte Church

Stop having a go at me 'cos it's getting pathetic. First of all, it was quite funny — but now it's just pathetic and I'm going to knock her out if I ever see her.

CHARLOTTE CHURCH on Cheryl Cole

Madonna… euch, no thank you. I just think she's vile, hideous, a horrible human being with no redeeming qualities. There's nothing nice about her. I've never heard anyone say anything nice about her at all. Everyone that's ever met her she's been vile to. Vile, full of herself… it's unbelievable, and she gets away with it… it's like, how has this woman got away with it for so long?

BOY GEORGE

Boy George – he piled on the pounds when he gave up the smack, didn't he?

RICKY GERVAIS

You mean that fat dancer from Take That?

NOEL GALLAGHER on Robbie Williams

He's a great singer – but he's not the most masculine guy, is he?

ALEXANDER O'NEAL on Michael Jackson

You know, YOUR President, the one with the big ears – he ain't MY President – had that woman singing for him at his Inauguration. She's going to get her ass whooped… How dare Beyonce sing MY song that I been singing forever.

ETTA JAMES on Barack Obama and Beyonce

I'd rather be on stage with a pig – a duet with Jennifer Lopez and me just ain't going to happen.

MARIA CAREY

I wouldn't be surprised if she made that African boy she adopted into a coat and wore him for fifteen minutes, then threw it away.

MORRISSEY on Madonna

Not in this lifetime. Why? Because I'm the only one she hasn't done it to.

SHARON STONE on Madonna wanting to kiss her

Madonna, Madonna, Madonna. I'm sick of
hearing about Madonna.

WHOOPI GOLDBERG

The ultimate Britney experience would involve a hearing
loss on my part, and clothing loss on her part.

PATTON OSWALT

I was a fan of hers, back when she was popular.

MARIAH CAREY on Madonna

I saw the new show and I think if I was her producer I
would have a word with her… She need not swear so
much, she need not remind us all the time
that she's Welsh.

MICHAEL PARKINSON on Charlotte Church

I'd love to see you host a talk show. It would be
rubbish, but I'd watch.

JONATHAN ROSS to Damon Albarn

Madonna is going to play Joan of Arc. She is playing a virgin. You thought the special effects in *Independence Day* were amazing.

JAY LENO

The DVD of Mariah Carey's movie *Glitter* is coming out with bonus features. Maybe one of them will be a plot.

JOAN RIVERS

I think that he's a good melodist, but he's a wanker... He's obviously a completely dysfunctional character and a cretin but he happens to be a great melodist.

BONO on Chris Martin

Is he just doing a bad Elvis pout, or was he born that way?

FREDDIE MERCURY on Billy Idol

Madonna, best fucking live act? Fuck off. Since when has lip-synching been live? That's me off her fucking Christmas card list but do I give a toss? No.

ELTON JOHN at The Q Awards

His album was called "Bad" because there wasn't
enough room on the sleeve for "Pathetic".

PRINCE on Michael Jackson

I would never try to be like other actors and attempt
to make [music] myself. I mean, have you heard 30
Seconds to Mars?... Fucking awful, man!

ELIJAH WOOD on Jared Leto

The judge is trying to teach you a lesson, shut your
mouth and learn it! You are a bad mother, and so is
your mother! Get your shit together and take
care of your kids.

ROSEANNE BARR to Britney Spears

Fuck off Elton. I am 40 years younger than you and
have my whole life ahead of me!

LILY ALLEN to Elton John onstage at the GQ Awards

I could still snort you under the table.

ELTON JOHN to Lily Allen onstage at the GQ Awards

I've met Madonna a few times and she's highly intelligent, driven and lacking in humour.

JANET STREET-PORTER

She's so hairy. When she lifted up her arm, I thought it was Tina Turner in her armpit.

JOAN RIVERS on Madonna

She's rough. I can't understand why they are dating. She looks like a man. It must be a stunt. I just can't believe it's true.

KIAN EGAN on Spice Girl Mel C

She looks like a campaign poster for neglected horses.

FRANKIE BOYLE on Amy Winehouse

Armed with a wiggle and a Minnie Mouse squawk, she is coarse and charmless.

SHEILA JOHNSON on Madonna

At the Grammy Awards, Keith Richards became the first performer ever to accept a posthumous award in person.

JAY LENO

The idea that a piece of white trash could string three words together – even if they were faggot, bitch and dick – was obviously deeply impressive.

JULIE BURCHILL on Eminem

You walk out of the Amphitheatre after watching the Rolling Stones perform and suddenly the Chicago Stockyards smell clean and good by comparison.

TOM FITZPATRICK

It's fun doing that joke here but of course the danger is that it's been broadcast now and maybe Asher D or a member of the So Solid Crew has seen that, and if you are Asher D or a member of the So Solid Crew, watching tonight then: yes I AM disrespecting you. I am disrespecting you to the max. Maximum disrespect.

STEWART LEE

If you really want to torture me, sit me in a room strapped to a chair and put Mariah Carey's records on.

CAMERON DIAZ

Pete Doherty creates all this misery for himself to write songs and then doesn't even turn up to play them. And they're not that good anyway.

CHARLOTTE CHURCH

She is the nastiest person I have ever seen.

CHRISTINA AGUILERA on Kelly Osbourne

I've seen drag queens who look better. She has a bad mouth on her, but she's all talk.

KELLY OSBOURNE on Christina Aguilera

She has ripped me off. We work with the same people, she married a Brit, she's got long hair and she likes fashion.

MADONNA on Gwen Stefani

It looks like she got it on QVC. She's not trailer trash, but she sure acts that way.

CHRISTINA AGUILERA on Britney Spears' engagement ring

from Kevin Federline

It was with great pride and enthusiasm that I took on management of the Pumpkins back in October, but unfortunately I must resign today due to medical reasons – Billy Corgan was making me sick!

SHARON OSBOURNE

He [Mick Jagger] seems to be a bit of a social climber. Wants to be part of the aristocracy. Like that twat out of Roxy Music, Bryan Ferry. Him and Jagger are always up some lord or lady's arsehole on a fucking Persian rug. They make me sick.

SHARON OSBOURNE

Is she a ho? She used to say she was a virgin.

AVRIL LAVIGNE on Britney Spears

I'd like her just to wash her hair. I'm going
to start small.

KATHY GRIFFIN on Britney Spears

I don't want to look like Britney Spears. She's hideous.

BETH DITTO

Congrats on your album doing well in America, though.
It's REALLY HARD to sell copies when u discount it to
$3.99. Desperate!

PEREZ HILTON to Lily Allen (on Twitter)

Sting is always boasting about his eight hours a night
sex sessions with his wife Trudi. Imagine how long he
could last if she was a looker.

JIMMY CARR

I thought Kanye West was a tube station near Uxbridge.

JONATHAN ROSS

I'm so glad Courtney Love is here; I left my crack in my other purse.

SARAH SILVERMAN

Rod Stewart is a man of principle; he will not go out with a woman with brown hair.

DAVID WALLIAMS

Her voice sounded like an eagle being goosed.

RALPH NOVAK on Yoko Ono

She looks like a cross between someone in a gay club at six in the morning and someone who's trying to save trees.

ROBBIE WILLIAMS on Christina Aguilera

Kids listening to Dido, thinking, "I want to be like her" makes me want to vomit.

AMY WINEHOUSE

She dances in the dark — and dresses there, too.

RICHARD BLACKWELL on Bjork

Shrink-wrapped cheesecake.

RICHARD BLACKWELL on Mariah Carey

If you want a piece of this business, you have to be able to deal with it. You can't complain about the pressures, the paparazzi, the madness because that's the job.

AVRIL LAVIGNE on Britney Spears

I met Courtney Love and she said she'd like to sleep with me, but couldn't because of my pop star thing. So I said I couldn't sleep with her either because of the ugly thing.

ROBBIE WILLIAMS

He's a fat dancer from Take That. Somebody who danced for a living! Stick to what you're good at, that's what I always say.

NOEL GALLAGHER on Robbie Williams

If him and his gawky bird want to go banging on about the war they can do it at their own gigs. That lot are just a bunch of knobhead students.

LIAM GALLAGHER on Chris Martin and Coldplay

There's no beginning to their talents.

CLIVE ANDERSON on the Bee Gees

I'm writing Kylie Minogue's biography. It's called *Superstar – Jesus Christ*!

BARRY CRYER

I'd do anything so as not to end up looking like him. I couldn't bear to look at myself in the mirror if I had to have my father staring back at me.

MICHAEL JACKSON

I feel sorry for Madonna, because she doesn't know who she is. That's why she dyes her hair so much. She tries to steal other people's identities.

SANDRA BERNHARD

I don't think that Michael Jackson thinks that dressing like Harry Potter will get him off. But I'm pretty certain that Michael Jackson thinking about Harry Potter gets him off.

JESSI KLEIN

US Weekly has reported that Britney has laid down an ultimatum. Either Kevin starts respecting Britney and their baby or he only gets like five or six more chances and then she's gonna' lay down another ultimatum.

NICK KROLL

I think Robbie Williams is a fucking asshole. I think he is a very misguided, easily led, stupid, foolish young individual who'd benefit from a slapping. I'd probably kick him down the stairs a couple of times, but I'm not a violent person and I don't like confrontation.

NOEL GALLAGHER

Can we not give her credit for getting him in the car seat? Like, just a couple weeks ago, she had him on the hood. Baby steps, people.

PAUL F. TOMPKINS on Britney Spears

I can hear Dietrich screaming from her grave, "Kill that trash".

SANDRA BERNHARD on Madonna

She used to do songs like "Papa Don't Preach" but now it's just "Fuck me, fuck me, fuck me".

SIR-MIX-ALOT on Madonna

I suppose Duff could play guitar on something somewhere but there's zero possibility of me having anything to do with Slash....In a nutshell, personally I consider him a cancer and better removed, avoided, and the less anyone heard of him or his supporters the better.

AXL ROSE on former bass player Duff McKagan

Getting married is the most fun you can have in life. Being married sucks.

KID ROCK on Pamela Anderson

Will Smith don't got to cuss in his raps to sell records —
well I do, so fuck him and fuck you too.

EMINEM

I'm a skinnier version of Lily Allen and a fatter version
of Amy Winehouse.

KATY PERRY

Really overweight girls or guys with lots of acne follow
me around and pester me. It's frightening because, not
only are they bothering me, but they're horrible
to look at too.

MADONNA on some of her fans

You have to admire Madonna. She hides her lack of
talent so well.

MANOLO BLAHNIK

. . . a crass social climber and a tramp.

JACKIE ONASSIS on Madonna

With lips like those, Mick Jagger could French-kiss
a moose.

JOAN RIVERS

I just don't like her as a person. I learned a lesson from
it [their "relationship"] – don't believe the hype… she
doesn't really have it all together.

EMINEM on Mariah Carey

While we appreciate Eminem as an artist, lately his
work has seemed tasteless and unnecessarily mean-
spirited. The public seems to agree – just look at his
declining record and concert ticket sales.

Mariah Carey's manager BENNY MEDINA

I love his work but I couldn't warm to him even if I was
cremated next to him.

KEITH RICHARDS on Chuck Berry

Sting — where is thy death?
JOE QUEENAN

He sounds like he's got a brick dangling from his willy, and a food-mixer making purée of his tonsils.
PAUL LESTER on Jon Bon Jovi

To Noel Gallagher, RIP. Heard your latest album — with deepest sympathy, Robbie Williams.
ROBBIE WILLIAMS, written on funeral wreath following poor reviews of Oasis' album Standing On The Shoulder Of Giants

He could be a manoeuvring swine, which no one ever realized.
PAUL McCARTNEY on John Lennon

A knobhead… looks like a dustbin man these days.
NOEL GALLAGHER on Damon Albarn

I just want to sock her!

MACY GRAY on Mariah Carey

His charity efforts? Mmmm. I'm sure they have nothing to do with his molestation charges.

CHRISTIAN FINNEGAN on Michael Jackson

Carrie Fisher was James Blunt's landlady and let him make a single in her bathroom. If James Blunt ever asks to use your bathroom, make sure he's only having a shit.

MARK LAMARR

He has a woman's name and wears makeup.
How original.

ALICE COOPER on Marilyn Manson

Peter Andre: the most unwelcome comeback since Jimi Hendrix's vomit.

MARK LAMARR

It's not very inspiring when you're just taking the music from old songs.

MADONNA on P. Diddy

If you're a common-or-garden homosexual then maybe, but not if you're a fag like I am. I'm not an Elton John type of gay. I'm not vanilla.

BOY GEORGE on whether Elton John is a gay role model

Hold your stomach in.

GAVIN HENSON to his wife Charlotte Church

With his womanly voice, stark white skin and Medusa hair, his gash of red lipstick, heavy eyeliner, almost nonexistent nose and lopsided face, Jackson was making his TV appearance in order to scotch all rumours that he is not quite normal.

CRAIG BROWN

Michael Bolton sounds like he's having his teeth drilled by Helen Keller.

JEFF WILDER

Cut off his nose to spite his race.

MARVIN GAYE on Michael Jackson

The latest rumour is that Britney Spears is pregnant again. It turns out it was not planned. She said it happened from sitting on a limo seat.

JAY LENO

Michael Jackson has introduced his own line of candy. It's white chocolate with a nut inside.

DAVID LETTERMAN

In rock, you're nothing until you've slept with Winona Ryder.

COURTNEY LOVE

She's angry because I have a natural nose and
she doesn't.

MADONNA on Janet Jackson

He could use my help. The last album was terrible. He's
at that point where he's just throwing anything out.
That new thing he's got out, it makes Ronan Keating
look like a genius.

BOY GEORGE on Robbie Williams

Gareth Gates went out with Jordan, which is the
dictionary definition of tit for tat.

MARK LAMARR

Pete grabbed the microphone and started singing.
Well, when I say singing, I mean he began emitting
a tuneless, whining noise more akin to a live lobster
being brought to the boil.

PIERS MORGAN on Pete Doherty

Michael Jackson was inducted into the Rock and Roll
Hall of Fame. It caused quite a controversy, because
his nose isn't eligible for another fifteen years.

CONAN O'BRIEN

The recording artist once named Pink will be called
"Beige" when people realize that that's the colour you
get when you mix her name with the crap she records.

JACK BLACK on Pink

Barry Manilow's singing sounds like a bluebottle
caught in the curtains.

JEAN ROOK

Liam Gallagher's going around the clubs saying
he's going to rearrange David Gest's face. I think
somebody's already done that.

GREG BURNS

Ashlee Simpson has announced that she's interested in being an interior designer. She says she want to prove to everyone that there are other things she's not good at.

CONAN O'BRIEN

Peter Andre's got two million fans. Imagine the draught if he turned them all on at once.

ALLY ROSS

The bland leading the blind.

ANTHONY BURGESS on Madonna

He of the tight smile, the high waistband and the oil slick charm.

PATRICK COLLINS on Simon Cowell

I got a message from Aretha Franklin saying she'd love to do a song with me. Later, after she'd done the [duet] with George Michael, the London *Evening Standard* asked me if I thought she'd called the wrong George. I said "I think she banged on the wrong closet."

BOY GEORGE

Dave Gahan of Depeche Mode has a pierced perineum, which is the bit between the scrotum and the arsehole. Just think Sharon Osbourne in between Louis Walsh and Simon Cowell.

MARK LAMARR

If I found her floating in my pool, I'd punish my dog.

JOAN RIVERS on Yoko Ono

There's a central dumbness to her.

MICK JAGGER on Madonna

I'm glad she doesn't like me. I only pity her. She's a virus. I don't want her anywhere near people I love.

SHARON OSBOURNE on Courtney Love after she allegedly introduced her son Jack to the drug OxyContin at the age of 15

It would be awful to be like Keith Richards. He's pathetic. It's like a monkey with arthritis trying to go on stage and look young.

ELTON JOHN

His writing is limited to songs for dead blondes.

KEITH RICHARDS on Elton John

George is in a strange place. There seems to be a deep-rooted unhappiness in his life and it shows on the album. All I would say to George is: you should get out more.

ELTON JOHN to George Michael

Boy George is all England needs – another queen who can't dress.

JOAN RIVERS

He moves like a parody between a majorette girl and Fred Astaire.

TRUMAN CAPOTE on Mick Jagger

Keith Richards looks like death warmed over.

JOE PISCOPO

She is closer to organized prostitution than anything else.

MORRISSEY on Madonna

I couldn't stand Janis Joplin's voice… She was just a screaming little loudmouthed chick.

ARTHUR LEE

The most over-rated person in pop history.

LILY ALLEN on Madonna

I dislike Victoria Beckham. I dislike the entitlement, the blunt total entitlement. You want to say "calm down, you were a Spice Girl". The arrogance when she walks into a room is astonishing.

JOAN RIVERS

Madonna said at her concert, Everyone needs to see *Fahrenheit 9/11*; now if you'll excuse me: I need to grind on this pregnant backup dancer.

JOHN ABOUD

David has more images than any singer, ever! He can be anybody, because at heart he's nobody.

KEITH MOON on David Bowie

Valentine's Day is the day you should be with the person you love the most. I understand Simon Cowell spent the day alone.

JAY LENO

Ages ago, Louis Walsh said he hated me and he thought I sucked. Two years later I was in the same room as him and he didn't even have the balls to introduce himself to me. He said "hello" to every single member of my family except me. I think he's a spineless prick.

KELLY OSBOURNE

Simon is a pompous little prick who walks like he has a stick stuck up his arse.

SHARON OSBOURNE on Simon Cowell

When has Pink not been copying me, in her fashion and so on? It's always like "Gosh, I just wore that last week".

CHRISTINA AGUILERA

Mick Jagger is now at that awkward age between being a Stone and passing one.

JAY LENO

She's got a face like a satellite dish and ankles like my granny's.

ROBBIE WILLIAMS on Sophie Ellis Bextor

Babyshambles have only ever released one song — one song! People talk about this great talent, but there's nothing to him. He's a mess.

DAMON ALBARN on Pete Doherty

He's so self-important and takes himself far too seriously. He doesn't publicise that he's got a two-million quid house in Battersea and all that.

LILY ALLEN on Bob Geldof

Madonna is mutton dressed as lamb. She's just not relevant now.

PEACHES GELDOF

Mariah Carey gets her dressing room repainted! I would never do that. What proper singer would?

SHIRLEY BASSEY

She's a lonely bitch… Did I tell you about my
nightmare? I dreamt I was Madonna, shopping at
Tiffany's, where I was trying to buy some class.

SANDRA BERNHARD

She is the worst possible Italian-American role model.
At least since Al Capone and that ilk.

DON AMECHE on Madonna

I heard Michael Jackson is moving to France. For the
first time my sympathies are with the French people.

BOY GEORGE

No wonder Bob Geldof's such an expert on famine –
he's been dining out on "I Don't Like Mondays" for
thirty years.

RUSSELL BRAND

Even her becoming a mother looks like a calculated career move.

ALAN J PAKULA on Madonna

Michael Jackson announced that he wants to record a song for the victims of Hurricane Katrina. Michael said if he could touch just one child…

JAY LENO

He's got a chin like an ironing board.

PETE BURNS on Lionel Richie

When you eat a lot of spicy food, you can lose your taste. When I was in India last summer, I was listening to a lot of Michael Bolton.

JIMMY CARR

I don't know why Shirley Bassey's always so nasty about me. I mean, she's a bit wrinkly, isn't she? She has a cheek. She's always drinking champagne. She needs to shut up. I have met her, she was OK, but rude.

CHARLOTTE CHURCH

I've never bought a Bob Dylan record. A singing poet? It just bores me to tears.

SIMON COWELL

Their public persona is now of a bunch of grumpy old men.

NOEL GALLAGHER on The Arctic Monkeys

He was so mean it hurt him to go to the bathroom.

BRITT EKLAND on Rod Stewart

It's all pose. It's all fucking posing. It's nothing to do with music. He knows it too.

KEITH RICHARDS on David Bowie

Overrated. He's marginally talented, but not anywhere near as good as me. If he wasn't shagging a supermodel, no one outside of NME would give a shit about him.

NOEL GALLAGHER on Pete Doherty

Razorlight disgust me. Johnny Borrell… comes across as a bit of a knob.

PEACHES GELDOF

I think he sounds like some weird guy with fuzzy hair from the seventies.

ALISON GOLDFRAPP on James Blunt

Hear'Say are the ugliest band I have ever seen. That guy Danny looks like Shrek.

ELTON JOHN

As he tends to refer to himself in the third person, Robbie Williams is obviously a character that he's invented and the music he makes is shit.

NOEL GALLAGHER

It's like they say, if you're rich and white, you can get away with anything.

JIMMY KIMMEL on Michael Jackson

A baroque art-rock bubblegum broadcast on a frequency understood only by female teenagers and bred field mice.

MARK COLEMAN on Duran Duran

Wham split over the Gulf War — the gulf in talent between them.

MARK LAMARR

Madonna is like a McDonald's hamburger. When you ask for a Big Mac you know exactly what you're getting. It's enjoyable, but it satisfies only for the moment.

SADE

There were little boys around the house all the time... As far as his sexual (orientation), he has never had a girlfriend, ever!

LA TOYA JACKSON on Michael Jackson

Joss Stone recently had to duet with Robbie Williams at the Brits. The only way I'd duet with Robbie Williams is on a tandem parachute jump. As long as I had the parachute and he had the tandem.

MARK LAMARR

I'm more about a performance, she's more about entertainment and sex, being a sex symbol and trying to look like she's having sex.

AVRIL LAVIGNE on Britney Spears

Mariah Carey, who checked into hospital for extreme exhaustion, is doing better. Her condition has been upgraded from serious to slightly self-indulgent.

JAY LENO

He plays four-and-a-half-hour sets. That's torture. Does he hate his audience?

JOHN LYDON on Bruce Springsteen

Jennifer Lopez has got engaged again. She's an amazing woman. She has movies coming out, she has CDs, she has concerts, she has her own perfume line, yet she still finds time two or three times a year to get married.

JAY LENO

He looks like a dwarf who's been dipped in a bucket of pubic hair.

BOY GEORGE on Prince

The easiest way for you to lose ten pounds is to just take off your wig.

MADONNA to Elton John

Michael Bolton said yesterday he now wants to become an opera singer. Which is great, because now my Dad and I can hate the same kind of music.

CONAN O'BRIEN

Michael Jackson is at home recovering from a broken foot. He can't perform. You know what you call a Jackson who can't perform? LaToya.

JAY LENO

Beyonce is a bitch. I only hope she gets bit on the arse by whatever animal she wears.

PINK

All legs and hair with a mouth that could swallow the whole stadium and the hot-dog stand.

LAURA LEE DAVIES on Tina Turner

Frank Zappa couldn't write a decent song if you gave him a million and a year on an island in Greece.

LOU REED

Madonna is a no-talent. She slept with everybody on the way up. That's how she made it to the top.

LA TOYA JACKSON

Britney Spears is a joke now. I wish her luck with her marriage as I hope it stops her going into the studio.

AMY WINEHOUSE

If you have to take heroin to be famous, well, I don't get it. Will Pete be a Kurt Cobain or a Jimi Hendrix? Never in a million years. He hasn't the talent to tune their guitars.

PETE WATERMAN on Pete Doherty

Actually, I never liked Dylan's kind of music before; I always thought he sounded just like Yogi Bear.

MIKE RONSON on Bob Dylan

It's a good thing we don't live in the United States, where guns are accessible, because I'd have blown his head off by now. The problem is, I can't fire him because my mum would kill me.

NOEL GALLAGHER on brother Liam

Long live the dullards like James Blunt. There are some wretched, talentless fools among the current crop of stars, whose records ought to be melted down and used to build vinyl rafts, upon which they should be set adrift in shark-infested waters.

JUSTIN HAWKINS

I think Mick Jagger would be astounded and amazed if he realized to how many people he is not a sex symbol but a mother image.

DAVID BOWIE

Celine Dion is moving to Belgium to prepare for her comeback tour. Belgium had announced it's moving to France.

CONAN O'BRIEN

If I were in the Beatles, I'd be a good George Harrison.

NOEL GALLAGHER

He makes Paul Simon look like LL Cool J.

IAN GITTINS on Art Garfunkel

I fucking despise hip hop. Loathe it. Eminem is a fucking idiot and I find 50 Cent the most distasteful character I have ever crossed in my life.

NOEL GALLAGHER

He is a mentally disturbed young man. He's out to lunch. You can't take his music seriously. He sings songs about oral sex and incest. It's my job to keep reality over this science fiction creep.

RICK JAMES on Prince

I'm not the biggest fan of Elvis Presley. He's all right, he gets the job done. But he's not quite 50 Cent or Eminem.

ANDY MURRAY

Even the deaf would be traumatized by prolonged exposure to the most hideous croak in Western culture. Richards's voice is simply horrible.

NICK COLEMAN on Keith Richards

I understand he represents the ugliness of this business. But he also represents questioning the dream, the American dream. Not just questioning it. Crushing it. Whereas I'm about hope.

PAULA ABDUL on Simon Cowell

Kylie Minogue is just a demonic little idiot as far as I'm concerned. She gets cool dance producers to work with her for some bizarre reason, I don't know why. She doesn't even have a good name. It's a stupid name, Kylie, I just don't get it.

NOEL GALLAGHER

Keep booing girl, I will punch a man with glasses.

EMINEM to Moby at the Video Music Awards 2002

Calling your child Apple? He's terribly vain. I think he has a narcissism complex. He wants to be Bono but he bleats in interviews about being "ubiquitous". Make your fucking mind up.

JUSTIN HAWKINS on Chris Martin

He reminds me of fucking Right Said Fred. You put
on I'm Too Sexy for my fucking shirt and I bet you any
money it's the same person. He's just gone on the
Atkins diet and grown his hair!

NOEL GALLAGHER on Alex Kapranos

I bet if he heard his stuff he'd be like:
"Who is that wanker?"

AMY WINEHOUSE on Chris Martin

She is one of the most disgusting human beings in the
entire world......I've seen drag queens who look better.

KELLY OSBOURNE on Christina Aguilera

Michael Jackson was a poor black boy who grew up to
be a rich white woman.

MOLLY IVENS

. . . about as sexy as a Venetian blind.

MADONNA on Sinéad O'Connor

I still love George Harrison as a songwriter in the Beatles, but as a person I think he's a fucking nipple. And if I ever meet him I'll fucking tell him.

AMY WINEHOUSE

The Band is now basically a T-Shirt selling machine. Jumping Jack Flash no more – more like Limping Hack Flash.

JULIE BURCHILL on The Rolling Stones

Just because you sell lots of records it doesn't mean to say you're any good. Look at Phil Collins.

NOEL GALLAGHER

Walking onstage at Reading with his bag of fucking Anadins and a bottle of Bacardi which is actually a bottle of water! I stood on the side of the stage thinking "You fucking knobhead".

AMY WINEHOUSE on Eminem

Boys, your regurgitated indie rock days are numbered so get over yourselves.

LILY ALLEN on Carl Barat and The Kooks

Kylie playing Glastonbury would be the ultimate insult.

LILY ALLEN

Busted are ugly; they've all got acne and wear more make-up than I do. They're the stupidest, most ridiculous fools ever.

KELLY OSBOURNE

I look at my friendship with her as like having a gall stone. You deal with it, there is pain, and then you pass it. That's all I have to say about Schmadonna.

SANDRA BERNHARD on Madonna

She must think it's her fucking lucky day... She's singing shit new songs that her manager writes for her.

AMY WINEHOUSE on Katie Melua

They can't sing. They suck big oranges.

RICK JAMES on Vanity 6

What an old bastard. He's a 60-year-old man who said three times he hates me. Anyone who uses "hate" that much needs help.

KELLY OSBOURNE on Louis Walsh

The towel bills that David Bowie must run up dyeing his hair.

ELTON JOHN

Razorlight? I don't really know and I don't want to. The only people I can think of worth speaking about are me and Winehouse, not boring Rae or Bedingfield. Whatever.

LILY ALLEN

I look at someone like Peter and I just think, "You're a fucking moron because your music was so much better before you started doing that". It's working in the sense that people want to come and look at the car crash.

JOHNNY BORRELL on Pete Doherty

He's not a musician. He's a critic… he's an NME reader, i.e., a useless fucking loser.

JUSTIN HAWKINS on Frankie Poullain

I only have one thing to say about that man – John Lydon is the devil in my eyes.

KELE OKEREKE

We have no time for him. Music is an art but he doesn't appreciate music for what it is. He started it. It shows what a bitter old man he has become.

ANDREW WHITE on Noel Gallagher

Liam is rude, arrogant, intimidating and lazy. He's like a man with a fork in a world of soup.

NOEL GALLAGHER on brother, Liam

Frank Zappa is the most untalented musician I've ever heard… He can't play rock 'n' roll because he's a loser.

LOU REED

Fame has sent a number of celebrities off the deep end, and in the case of Michael Jackson, to the kiddy pool.

BILL MAHER

He isn't really interested in music… he's using music for ammunition.

JOHN CALE on Frank Zappa

She made a movie. It came and went, right? It at least proved she can't act either.

CAMERON DIAZ on Britney Spears

If you want to be a household name, be a household name… if you're concerned about fair trade, tattoo it on your skin, don't just fucking write it on your hand in felt tip.

JUSTIN HAWKINS on Chris Martin

Andrew Lloyds Webber's music is everywhere, but so is AIDS.

MALCOLM WILLIAMSON

[People] always go on about "theatre is a dying art form and we must save it", and then we just put on another Andrew Lloyd Webber re-run. It's tragic.

BOY GEORGE

It looks as though the plastic surgery has left Gest closely resembling the halfway point in a horror movie transformation sequence.

CHARLIE BROOKER on David Gest

Somebody should clip Sting around the head and tell him to stop using that ridiculous Jamaican accent.

ELVIS COSTELLO

Things that look better than the Spice Girls: loft lagging, a bucket of slops, and a waxwork model of Bill Bailey that's been left by the radiator.

MARK LAMARR

I think Oasis are the most over-rated and pernicious band of all time. They had a totally negative and dangerous impact upon the state of British music. They have made stupidity hip.

JUSTIN HAWKINS

ROYALTY

The Queen has no fashion sense. She's the richest woman in the world and look how she dresses. She wears soap-on-a-rope for jewellery.

JOAN RIVERS

It is time to send him back to Germany from where he comes. You want to know his original name? It ends with Frankenstein.

MOHAMED AL FAYED on the Duke of Edinburgh

We are all probably related to the Royal Family because they put it about so much over the last 1,000 years.

KEN LIVINGSTONE on Boris Johnson's discovery that he is an illegitimate descendant of George II

I am the only woman who has not been beheaded for leaving the Royal Family.

SARAH FERGUSON, Duchess of York

. . . that young twerp.

Labour MP WILLIE HAMILTON on Prince Charles

A very pleasant middle to upper-class type lady with a talkative retired Navy husband.

MALCOLM MUGGERIDGE on the Queen

I thought it was sad, you know that they had that pop concert to commemorate Diana. I mean, she didn't have much to do with pop music did she? They should have done something that celebrated what was really great about her life by staging a gang-bang in a minefield.

FRANKIE BOYLE on Princess Diana

For fifty years or more, Elizabeth Windsor has maintained her dignity, her sense of duty – and her hairstyle.

HELEN MIRREN, Oscars acceptance speech

Who wants to be photographed with a Queen who looks
like she's dressed in 1980s Marks & Spencer? She
should be stuck into a corset, plucked and dressed,
given some heels and pushed out there
doing it. She is appalling.

BOY GEORGE on the Queen

He rarely lifts a finger unless it's to feel up a cheap tart
in a nightclub.

CAROL SARLER on Prince Harry

The only constants in the blindingly mediocre life of
Princess Margaret would appear to be privilege, illness
and lashings of alcohol.

TONY PARSONS

My husband is planning an accident in my car, brake failure and serious head injury in order to make the path clear for him to marry Tiggy. Camilla is nothing more than a decoy.

DIANA SPENCER in a letter read at her inquest

Princess Ann is so outdoorsy. She loves nature in spite of what nature did to her.

BETTE MIDLER

Diana was never a fashion icon. She dressed to the same demotic standard of elegance as TV anchorwomen do, plus the inevitable hat. This was a desperate woman seeking applause. In death she has it, doled out in huge amounts.

GERMAINE GREER on Diana Spencer

Prince Charles is the only member of the Royal Family
who ever left Cinderella for the Ugly Duckling.

DES HANAFIN

Apparently Diana was assassinated by the provisional
wing of Interflora in an effort to boost sales.

RICHARD SKEEN

Have you ever flown in a plane? Well, it was
just like that.

DUKE OF EDINBURGH when asked "how was your flight?"

So, who's on drugs here? He looks as if he's on drugs.

**DUKE OF EDINBURGH singles out 14-year-old Shahin Ullah during a
royal visit to a Bangladeshi youth club in Central London**

The bastards murdered half my family.

**DUKE OF EDINBURGH on the Russian people during a royal
visit to Russia**

It will never work with all those Huns, wops and dagos.

The QUEEN MOTHER on the European Union

The Princess is vivid proof that we end up with the
appearance we deserve. She looks what she is, which
is a bitter, unhappy, selfish, old woman.

LYNDA LEE-POTTER on Princess Margaret

Queen Elizabeth II is head of a dysfunctional family.
If she lived on a council estate in Sheffield, she'd
probably be in council care.

MICHAEL PARKINSON

So you sponge off him them?

DUKE OF EDINBURGH to Simon Cowell on Paul Potts

I'm prepared to take advice on leisure from Prince Philip. He's a world expert on leisure. He's been practising for most of his adult life.

NEIL KINNOCK on the Duke of Edinburgh

She is a lady short on looks, absolutely deprived of any dress sense, has a figure like a Jurassic monster… very greedy when it comes to loot, no tact and wants to upstage everyone else.

SIR NICHOLAS FAIRBAIRN on Sarah Ferguson

Anybody else here? Ah, our little Paki friend… Ahmed.

PRINCE HARRY on fellow Sandhurst recruit, Ahmed Raza Khan

It's Dan the Man. Fuck me, you look like a raghead!

PRINCE HARRY on another fellow Sandhurst recruit

If you stay here much longer, you'll all be slitty-eyed.

DUKE OF EDINBURGH to a group of British students during

a state visit to China

How do you keep the natives off the booze long enough
to get them through the test?

DUKE OF EDINBURGH to a driving instructor in Oban, Scotland

Still throwing spears?

DUKE OF EDINBURGH to an Australian Aborigine

It looks as if it was put in by an Indian.

DUKE OF EDINBURGH about an old-fashioned fuse box in a factory

near Edinburgh

You are a woman, aren't you?

DUKE OF EDINBURGH to a Kenyan woman

If it has got four legs and it is not a chair, if it has got two wings and it flies but is not an aeroplane, and if it swims and it is not a submarine, the Cantonese will eat it.

DUKE OF EDINBURGH at a World Wildlife Fund meeting

You managed not to get eaten, then?

DUKE OF EDINBURGH to a student who had been trekking in Papua New Guinea

The idea of Prince Charles conversing with vegetables is not quite so amusing when you remember that he's had plenty of practice chatting to members of his own family.

JACI STEPHENS

Poor, pathetic creature isn't he? A man in his fifties who still calls his mother "mummy."

CLARE RAYNER on Prince Charles

SPORT

Football's a difficult business, and aren't they prima donnas?

QUEEN ELIZABETH II

Stone me! We've had cocaine, bribery and Arsenal scoring two goals at home. But just when you thought there were no surprises left in football, Vinnie Jones turns out to be an international player.

JIMMY GREAVES

He's six-foot something, fit as a flea, good-looking – he's got to have something wrong with him. Hopefully he's hung like a hamster! That would make us all feel better!

IAN HOLLOWAY on Cristiano Ronaldo

Paul Scholes can't score goals any more and looks like a gonk with a French crop.

TIM LOTT

My dad always taught me to respect my elders, but the old man's going to get battered on Saturday night for twelve rounds.

JOE CALZAGHE on Bernard Hopkins

He hasn't got the best teeth in the world but you can afford to go and get them done now if you like.

CLAIRE BALDING to Grand National Winner Liam Treadwell

If it had been a cheese roll it would never have got past him.

GRAHAM GOOCH on Shane Warne's "ball of the century" which Mike Gatting missed

Without being too harsh on David, he cost us the match.

IAN WRIGHT on David Beckham

Hate is a very strong word. I just despise her to the maximum level just below hate. I'm going to serve it right at the body, about 128 [mph], right into her midriff. If she's not crying by the time she comes off court then I did not do my job.

Senior ATP official JUSTIN GIMELSTOB on an exhibition match with Anna Kournikova

She wouldn't make any noise during sex. I can't tell you how disappointed I was. I really thought, like a lot of guys, that she'd be the loud screaming type. But instead, she just lay there like a dead frog. She even got angry if I started to moan, said it "ruined her concentration".

ADAM LEVINE on Maria Sharapova

I don't want to be rude, but I think when God gave him his enormous footballing talent, he took his brain out at the same time to sort of equalise it a bit.

TONY BANKS on Paul Gascoigne

Maybe he wants to go into the movies; if they are silent movies, he has a good chance.

MAX CLIFFORD on David Beckham's move to LA

She is a sexpot. She's a little sexpot. She's a well-developed young lady. She has a great body but her face is a five.

Senior ATP official JUSTIN GIMELSTOB on Tatiana Golovin, Alize Cornet, Nicole Vaidisova and Anna Kournikova

I'm particularly unimpressed with the big midfielder Effenberg who has been renamed in our house "Effenuseless".

PETER CORRIGAN on Stefan Effenberg

. . . the golliwog frog… well, he's half-golliwog… Now I'm in trouble, just like Prince Harry.

CAROLE THATCHER on French-Congolese tennis player

Jo-Wilfried Tsonga

We are not calling them the All Blacks this week. They are New Zealand, which is a poxy little island in the Pacific Ocean… I apologise to all New Zealanders. In fact, it's two islands.

Wales Assistant rugby coach SCOTT JOHNSON

Becks hasn't changed since I've known him – he's always been a flash Cockney git.

RYAN GIGGS on David Beckham

She shouldn't be here. I know that sounds sexist but I am sexist. This is not park football, so what are women doing here? If you start bringing in women you have big problems. It is tokenism for the politically correct idiots.

Luton manager MIKE NEWELL on assistant referee Amy Rayner

Pakistan is the sort of country to send your mother-in-law to.

IAN BOTHAM

As soon as I got on the green I was a spaz.

TIGER WOODS being un-PC

A man so dull he once made the papers for having a one-in-a-bed romp.

NICK HANCOCK on Alan Shearer

I speak my mind and other chairmen should too. They need to wake up from their coma. They can have lunch with me at Harrods, where I can serve them stags' testicles. We need big balls in this business.

MOHAMED AL-FAYED

Wenger signs hosts of players from France and elsewhere year in year out. We have to take care that this sort of child trafficking is stopped. The word kidnapping is not too far off any more.

Bayern Munich chairman KARL HEINZ RUMMENIGGE on Arsène Wenger

Who needs Lamborghinis and Ferraris? I've got two whippets and a ferret.

PAUL INGLE on Naseem Hamed

Comparing Gascoigne to Pele is like comparing Rolf Harris to Rembrandt.

RODNEY MARSH on Paul Gascoigne

Manchester is the city of rain. Its main attraction is considered to be the timetable at the railway station, where trains leave for other, less rainy cities.

NEMANJA VIDIC

They took Wembley stadium down but there's a little bit of ground with Colin Hendry still standing there.

PAUL GASCOIGNE on his famous goal against Scotland

I don't do men with breasts.

Painter JACK VETTRIANO on Colin Montgomerie

I don't think Lee Bowyer is racist at all; I think he would
stamp on anyone's head.

RODNEY MARSH

Just because you're paid £120,000 a week and do well
for 20 minutes against Spurs, you think you
are a superstar.

ROY KEANE on Rio Ferdinand

I just couldn't lose to a bloke wearing a shirt like that.

LLEYTON HEWITT on Dominik Hrbaty

You cannot keep your place because you look elegant at
the crease. A team of good-lookers won't win anything.

GEOFF BOYCOTT on Michael Vaughan

How do you still fight like a hungry man when your refrigerator's full?

BERNARD HOPKINS on Floyd Mayweather

Crouchy, when I look at you, everything tells me you should be rubbish at football.

JAMES CORDEN to Peter Crouch

Why do Mike Tyson's eyes water when he has sex? Mace.

JOHN CAMPONERA

To call Keegan a superstar is stretching a point. He's been very, very lucky, an average player who came into the game when it was short of personalities. He's not fit to lace my boots as a player.

GEORGE BEST on Kevin Keegan

He looks like a cross between a terminally ill school boy and a flamingo.

FRANKIE BOYLE on Peter Crouch

He could help to save human lives but instead he
chooses to advertise crisps. Why? Why does Gary
Lineker choose to advertise crisps? It can only be that
he is sexually aroused by the idea of obese
children dying.

STEWART LEE

John McCririck looks like Worzel Gummidge after an
incident with a letter bomb.

VICTOR LEWIS-SMITH

Poor lass she can't sing… I hope she doesn't sing in
the bath because it will keep him [David Beckham]
awake all bloody night.

BRIAN CLOUGH on Victoria Beckham

John McCririck looks like a hedge dragged through a
man backwards.

CLIVE JAMES

Ally MacLeod thinks that tactics are a new kind of mint.

BILLY CONNOLLY

When Peter Beardsley appears on television, daleks hide behind the sofa.

NICK HANCOCK

I've seen George Foreman shadow boxing and the shadow won.

MUHAMMAD ALI

I hate my muscles. I'm not Venus Williams. I'm not Serena Williams. I don't want to look like they look.

ANNA KOURNIKOVA

Beckham? His wife can't sing and his barber can't cut hair.

BRIAN CLOUGH

You can't see as well as these fucking flowers – and they're fucking plastic.

JOHN McENROE to a line judge

I've never met David Beckham, but I'm not in a trance about him like everybody else. I don't want him on my programme… I only want honest, feisty people with strong opinions.

PIERS MORGAN

Hijo de puta (son of a whore).

DAVID BECKHAM to a linesman, for which he received a red card

You look at Sven and you think… he's a pharmacist… he should be saying "Here's your pile ointment".

FRANK SKINNER on Sven-Göran Eriksson

He covers every blade of grass, but that's only because his first touch is crap.

DAVE JONES on Carlton Palmer

I once said Gazza's IQ was less than his shirt number and he asked me: "What's an IQ?"

GEORGE BEST

Kelly Holmes' outfit on Sunday looked like something a transvestite builder might favour.

MATTHEW NORMAN

McEnroe was as charming as always, which means that he was as charming as a dead mouse in a loaf of bread.

CLIVE JAMES

I'd hate to be next door to her on her wedding night.

PETER USTINOV on Monica Seles

Michael Owen – he's got the legs of a salmon.

CRAIG BROWN

There's nothing new you can say about Linford Christie – except, he's slow and has got a small penis.

NICK HANCOCK

He couldn't bowl a hoop downhill.

FRED TRUEMAN on Ian Botham

It's the best thing to happen to a sport, that you have
a superstar. In football there is always something to
write about the Beckhams, same as people want to
write about Rooney or Hooney or whatever his
bloody name is.

BERNIE ECCLESTON

I've never met her but everyone says she is really rude
and arrogant. If he's stuck with the shrew, I hope he
screws everything that's not tied down.

JOAN RIVERS on David and Victoria Beckham

To be fair to Henman, he was once the fourth in the
world, let's not forget… and reached six grand slam
finals, which is a great achievement for a
totally shit player.

FRANKIE BOYLE on Tim Henman

He's got a lot of forehead.

GARY LINEKER on Sven-Göran Eriksson

The other advantage England have got when Phil Tufnell is bowling is that he isn't fielding.

IAN CHAPPELL

The captain with a choirboy face and endearing tendency to drop easy catches.

STEPHEN MOSS on Michael Vaughan

Shane Warne's idea of a balanced diet is a cheeseburger in each hand.

IAN HEALEY

I think I've already made more tackles in one season of rugby than he did in his entire career. The bloke should go live in Holland and make his living as a windmill.

WENDELL SAILOR on David Campese

Alan Shearer, he's boring isn't he? We call him
Mary Poppins.

FREDDY SHEPHERD, the chairman of Newcastle United

Many people are bored to death by Jonny... If it was
meant to be a kicking game William Webb Ellis would
never have picked up the ball and ran with it in the
first place – that was the idea.

GRANT BATTY on Jonny Wilkinson

The mullet king.

CRIS FREDDI on Chris Waddle

I was thrilled until I learned Ivan Lendl had finished
above me.

ALLY McCOIST on learning he had come fifth in a list of

best-looking sportsmen

We all [players on the women's circuit] like each other
except Kournikova; no one likes her.

PATTY SCHNYDER

I'm not the next [Anna] Kournikova — I want to win matches.

MARIA SHARAPOVA

It's difficult to play against a man... I mean against Martina.

HANA MANDLIKOVA on Martina Navratilova

He is what John Major would be if he swallowed a bucket of Viagra.

PAUL HAYWARD on Sven-Göran Eriksson

For almost three sets, Roger Federer played his absolute worst, while Andy Roddick, the world's second-best player, played very nearly his best... and there was next to nothing to choose between them.

MATTHEW NORMAN

Sampras may be the greatest male tennis player ever, but... he is also one of the dullest human beings.

MATTHEW NORMAN

An orange crochet hussy dress modelled after something that Wilma Flintstone might choose… the stylistic equivalent of trash talk.

ROBIN GIVHAN on Serena Williams

The All-England Club… would have pitched him in the women's event were it not for the fear he might meet a Williams sister and have his spine snapped.

MARTIN SAMUEL on Tim Henman

If Tim Henman wins Wimbledon, I am going to do this show in one of Sue Barker's old dresses.

PAT CASH

It's difficult to cheer on someone who in your heart of hearts you know you could probably beat yourself.

FRANKIE BOYLE on Tim Henman

Tyneside's very own Renaissance man. A man capable of breaking both leg and wind at the same time.

JIMMY GREAVES on Paul Gascoigne

Can there ever have been a "sports personality" more
lacking in wit, charm, imagination and style than
Tim Henman?

BRYAN APPLEYARD

He cannot kick with his left foot, he cannot head a ball,
he cannot tackle and he doesn't score many goals.
Apart from that he's all right.

GEORGE BEST on David Beckham

This year… Henman is trying his very best to get
tough. He's grunting and growling and returning serve
with the kind of filthy looks he hasn't had cause to
throw since his wild teenage years when he threw a
strop over not being allowed to watch Pogle's Wood and
he had to be sent to bed without any tea.

AIDAN SMITH

He can make a five-set melodrama out of any
three-set stroll.

SIMON BARNES on Tim Henman

A lot of people are using two-piece cues nowadays. Alex Higgins hasn't got one because they don't come with instructions.

STEVE DAVIS

Sir Cliff Richard will never again be allowed to "entertain" the Centre Court crowd during a rain break… It is an indication of how traumatic his brief appearance was that many people think it is an annual occurrence.

EVE FODENS on the Wimbledon Centre Court sliding roof

The local [Barnsley] girls are far uglier than the ones in Belgrade. Our women are far prettier and they don't drink as much beer.

GEORGI HRISTOV

He's been the pain in my arse all my life.

PHIL TUFNEL on Shane Warne

He has a face like a warthog that's been stung by a wasp.

DAVID FEHERTY on Colin Montgomerie

John Barnes's problem is that he gets injured appearing on *A Question of Sport*.

TOMMY DOCHERTY

The biggest danger in fighting Bruno is that you might get hit by flying glass.

JIM MURRAY on Frank Bruno's infamous "glass jaw"

Chris Eubank lost his recent comeback fight on points… the main one being that he's a total git.

NICK HANCOCK

If a Frenchman goes on about seagulls, trawlers and sardines, he's called a philosopher. I'd just be called a short Scottish bum talking crap.

GORDON STRACHAN on Eric Cantona

Eighty percent of the top 100 women are fat pigs who don't deserve equal pay.

Tennis player RICHARD KRAJICEK

Lennox Lewis, I'm coming for you man. My style is impetuous. My defence is impregnable, and I'm just ferocious. I want your heart. I want to eat his children. Praise be to Allah!

MIKE TYSON

Trevor Brooking floats like a butterfly and stings like one too.

BRIAN CLOUGH

All praise is to Allah, I'll fight any man, any animal, if Jesus were here I'd fight him too.

MIKE TYSON on Jesus Christ

If David Seaman's dad had worn a condom, we'd still be in the World Cup.

NICK HANCOCK on England's defeat to Brazil in the 2002 World Cup

You're sweet. I'm going to make sure you kiss me good with those big lips. I'm gonna' make you my girlfriend.

MIKE TYSON on Razor Ruddock

If Tim Henman had won Wimbledon it would have been so weird it would have actually torn a hole in our reality… "here to present the trophy is Winston Churchill".

FRANKIE BOYLE on Tim Henman

After boxing, I would think Mike will resort to what he was doing when he was growing up – robbing people.

Former trainer TOMMY BROOKS on Mike Tyson

I still love Don, he's a great guy. But he's evil, and he steals people's money.

MIKE TYSON on Don King

Seb Coe is a Yorkshireman. So he's a complete bastard and will do well in politics.

DALEY THOMPSON

He is playing better and better, even if he is going grey and looking like a pigeon.

GIANLUCA VIALLI on Mark Hughes

Roy Keane has said that he will stay at Man United through thick and thin – or Becks and Posh, as they are known.

RORY BREMNER

Lee Bowyer is the nastiest piece of work in sport – a violent, foul-mouthed, horrible little lout.

PIERS MORGAN

Hard men? Well there was that picture of Vinnie Jones holding Gazza's wotsits. In my day we called someone who did that a poof.

GEORGE BEST

Being thick isn't an affliction if you're a footballer, because your brains need to be in your feet.

BRIAN CLOUGH on David Beckham

The last time I saw something that tall standing so still for so long, it was perched on the edge of a cliff shining a light across the sea.

DAVID ICKE on Emile Heskey

How much further down his head will Bobby Charlton have to part his hair before he faces the fact that he is bald?

CLIVE JAMES

I'm hoping Wayne Rooney might get injured, I've a little toy model of Shrek I've been sticking pins in all day.

RORY McGRATH

Somebody compared him to Billy McNeil, but I don't remember Billy being crap.

TOMMY DOCHERTY on Lorenzo Amoruso

That Seaman is a handsome young man but he spends too much time looking in his mirror, rather than at the ball. You can't keep goal with hair like that.

BRIAN CLOUGH on David Seaman

When the lad finishes playing he'd better have some savings, because he isn't going to have a second career, is he?

DAVID MELLOR on Wayne Rooney

Wayne didn't turn me on at all. He was ugly. He had a face like a smacked arse.

Prostitute GINA McCARRICK on Wayne Rooney

Rooney seems to have modelled his style of play on the baby elephant that ran amok in the Blue Peter studio. There is the same impossible size, and there is the same impossibly young age — Rooney is still only 18. There is the same air of not being quite in control, as if he hadn't yet got around to counting his limbs.

SIMON BARNES

Apparently Wayne Rooney's girlfriend Colleen is given to knocking back £200 bottles of Cristal… when a bottle or two of Mongolian Spumante would probably tickle their sophisticated palates just as nicely.

DAVID MELLOR

The only time he opens his mouth is to change feet.

DAVID FEHERTY on Nick Faldo

At least I have an identity; you're only Frances
Edmonds's husband.

Australia wicketkeeper TIM ZOEHRER to Phil Edmonds

They are precisely the kind of people that one would
dread as neighbours. They have lots of money
but no class.

DAME BARBARA CARTLAND on David and Victoria Beckham

David James must have a brain the size of a pea.
I called him a cretin a year ago so it has taken him
a whole year to find out the meaning of the word. My
two-year-old daughter could learn quicker than that.
In fact, people can go to university and do a whole
degree course in that time. He has learnt the
meaning of one or two words.

PAOLO DI CANIO

I hear Glen Hoddle has found God. That must have been one hell of a pass.

JASPER CARROTT

You were 33-1 to win the Six Nations this year. Now you are 16-1. If you can keep Henson out of Church going into it… what are the chances?

SUE BARKER on Gavin Henson and Charlotte Church

This is the same country that buys Mariah Carey records. It has nothing to do with art.

MADONNA on the O. J. verdict

The Queen Mother of football.

ARTHUR SMITH on Gary Lineker

I'm a lesbian trapped in a man's body.
A bit like Martina Navratilova.

EDDIE IZZARD and FRANK SKINNER

WAGS, SLAGS & CELEBUTANTES

Socialites and heiresses should shut the fuck up. Who the hell is Brandon Davis? He's a socialite. You know what that is, people? That's somebody rich that just hangs out.

MIKE BRITT

No one knows who you are. You're an old fucking singer no one knows about.

KATIE PRICE to Peter Andre

You can see what kind of a stupid, miserable, arrogant cow she is.

PETER ANDRE on Katie Price

Paris Hilton's new boyfriend doesn't know what she's going to give him for Valentine's Day but he hopes it won't require penicillin.

JOAN RIVERS

Is anybody really surprised there is another Paris Hilton sex tape? I bet if I look in my garage long enough, I will find a Paris Hilton sex tape.

MICHAEL COLTON

I have to recognize someone special here in the house. Perez Hilton, please stand up. We have the world's biggest douchebag asshole in the house!

CRISS ANGEL

I've made, like, $200 million in the last year, while J. Lo's only made $150 million so it's doing pretty well.

PARIS HILTON

You can only get so far without discernable talent — then you either work, or use cheap publicity tricks to keep the public's attention.

GEORGE CLOONEY on Paris Hilton

They dress down quite a lot here, don't they? It seems
to be in keeping to go to Starbucks in tracksuit
bottoms and Ugg boots.

VICTORIA BECKHAM on Hollywood women

. . . up herself.

CHERYL COLE on Peaches Geldoff

. . . like a builder's elbow.

JORDAN on Jodie Marsh's nose

. . . as hooked as a witch's.

JODIE MARSH on Jordan's nose

. . . like spaniel's ears.

JORDAN on Jodie Marsh's boobs

I hate the woman. She needs to get a job, put her tits away because they're horrible and get a nose job.

CHARLOTTE CHURCH on Rebecca Loos

The Burger Queen Sensation may be very rich – but she looks like yesterday's cheesecake… with a side of kitsch.

MR BLACKWELL on Paris Hilton

Jordan said that Gareth Gates was very inexperienced and didn't know where to put his hands. If anyone is in that position again: round her throat and squeeze 'til her eyes pop.

MARK LAMARR

It's disgusting. It reminds me of cottage cheese inside of a big trash bag.

PARIS HILTON on Kim Kardashian's ass

The woman is a ludicrous, hypocritical, shameless, grasping creature of such splendid, unrelenting awfulness that her very existence now brings daily joy to my life.

PIERS MORGAN on Heather Mills

Z-list personalities such as Vanessa Feltz come out with astoundingly self-pitying statements about how fame has ruined their lives, as if she hadn't pursued it with all the dignity of a rat up a drainpipe.

JULIE BURCHILL

Selfless is not the word that comes to mind about an acerbic woman who always seems most concerned with what she wants and rarely wastes time on anyone who isn't a hunk or useful.

LYNDA LEE-POTTER on Ulrika Jonsson

It's no big secret that Nicole and I are no longer friends. Nicole knows what she did, and that's all I'm ever going to say about it. Nicole cannot stand being around me, because I get all the attention and people really don't care about her.

PARIS HILTON on Nicole Richie

In life, you kind of press the delete button on the people that aren't good for you. She's no longer part of my life and I think that's much more important to her than it is to me.

NICOLE RICHIE on Paris Hilton

Why do they call you Posh?

NAOMI CAMPBELL to Victoria Beckham

Posh is stupid and thick. If anyone is a bitch, it's Victoria.

NAOMI CAMPBELL'S MUM on Victoria Beckham

A suicidal, silicone-breasted, bleached-blonde, 40-year-old mother of four, adulterous spawn of Hughie Green and a Bluebell Girl, with a dead boyfriend, an even deader career and a habit of being sick into her handbag at public parties.

JULIE BURCHILL on Paula Yates

You should try doing tomorrow's performance with your knickers on because it will help warm up your voice. You have a very bad vibe that comes from you.

SHARON OSBOURNE to Rebecca Loos

We both had affairs with married men – but at least mine was fit… Sharon seems to have forgotten how she got to where she is. What's she famous for? Being a rock star's wife.

REBECCA LOOS on Sharon Osbourne

I think the reason I never ended up in as much trouble as Paris or Lindsay seem to is that I'm not stupid, so I'd never do a lot of the things those girls do, and I've always had good friends around me. They need to straighten up a little bit and make better investments.

TARA REID on Paris Hilton and Lindsay Lohan

Apparently by the year 2020, the world's population will have increased by 20 percent. So the question is, how do we find Kerry Katona and stop her?

FRANKIE BOYLE

Why did God create the Paris Hilton sex videotape? So retarded people would have something to masturbate to.

NEIL HAMBURGER

I notice that the number of cosmetic-surgery operations has risen by 34 percent in the past year. Once we subtract Jordan, Jodie Marsh and Michael Jackson from those figures, we can see that demand overall may have stabilised.

MICHAEL GOVE

A recreation [prison] yard with the sun beating down on you is prematurely ageing. Take skin cream.

HEIDI FLEISS to Paris Hilton

We don't airbrush to that extent.

HUGH HEFNER on Kelly Osbourne's chances of posing for *Playboy*

I heard that to make her more comfortable in prison the guards are going to paint the bars to look like penises… I just worry that she's going to break her teeth on those things.

SARAH SILVERMAN on Paris Hilton

Oh, I'm sorry, we've already cast the jealous and bitter lonely old queen role. Next time eh?

LILY ALLEN to Perez Hilton (on Twitter)

I think she's jealous because I have a brain. I actually wrote my own book. She had to have someone write hers for her.

JODY MARSH on Jordan

Despite allegations of being thick, Jodie is a very successful glamour model. 36–24–32: no one's exactly sure what her IQ is.

ANGUS DEATON on Jodie Marsh

Jodie left school with eleven GCSEs and three A levels. I don't know whose they were but she left school with them.

ANGUS DEATON on Jodie Marsh

If you had to get someone to answer a question on a quiz machine to save your life... I would rather that she fell drunkenly on the quiz machine with her face and chose the answer that way.

FRANKIE BOYLE on Jodie Marsh

A lot of ass but so very little class.

IAN O'DOHERTY on Sadie Frost

A fat person pretending to be thin.

NORMAN PACE on Vanessa Feltz

You are what you eat? She looks like she's eaten Gollum off *Lord of the Rings*.

PAUL McKENNA on Gillian McKeith

Look at her. Shrill, nagging little face. In Ireland this is what we thought Protestants looked like when we were growing up. Really pale and miserable and going on at you.

DARA O'BRIAN on Gillian McKeith

Jo O'Meara looks uncannily like the bastard child of Pat Butcher and Vinnie Jones.

IAN O'DOHERTY

She's a professional slapper, which appears to be an actual career opportunity in England.

BRENDAN O'CONNOR on Jodie Marsh

Lindsay Lohan has got the stinkiest fucking sweaty orange fucking vagina anyone has ever seen. I haven't seen it. She wants me to see it, but it shits out freckles, it's orange and it fucking smells of diarrhoea.

BRANDON DAVIS

She was born with quite a lot going for her and she's screwed up quite a lot along the way and I think people find that irritating. She's a bit of a flibbertigibbet.

CHRISTINE HAMILTON on Tara Palmer-Tomkinson

Paris Hilton's feet are size eleven – almost as large as her mouth.

CINDY ADAMS

Peaches Geldof did this documentary about Islam and it was really awful. I watched her on *Richard and Judy*. She was like, "you know, I just really think that, like, kids in this country just like, don't know enough about Islam." What do you know about Islam, you useless oaf?

LILY ALLEN

Who let the dogs out? Woof, woof.

VICTORIA BECKHAM to Jordan

Posh has said to David Beckham that if she doesn't become a star in America in six months, she's going to try for another baby. I think they may as well start thinking of names.

GREG BURNS

The very epitome of global talentless celebrity.

PIERS MORGAN on Paris Hilton

It was reported last week that Paris Hilton doesn't pay for her drinks when she goes out. Don't worry, she's still getting plenty of fluids.

CONAN O'BRIEN

Heather Mills says she will never marry again. Three hundred million men can now uncross their legs and breathe a sigh of relief.

ALLISON PEARSON

Heather Mills is a liar. I wouldn't be surprised if we found out she's actually got two legs.

JONATHAN ROSS

Creating a cultural icon out of someone who goes, "I'm stupid, isn't it cute?" Makes me want to throw daggers.

REESE WITHERSPOON on Jessica Simpson

Abi Titmuss? She's been tied to more bedposts than David Blunkett's dog.

JONATHAN ROSS

Paris Hilton is reportedly upset because her private diaries have been stolen. Police say the suspect must have had access to her bedroom. So it could be anyone.

CONAN O'BRIEN

She can't even chew gum and walk in a straight line, let alone write a book.

AMY WINEHOUSE on Victoria Beckham

Lindsay Lohan is a firecrotch, she has freckles coming out of her vagina, and her clitoris is seven feet long.

BRANDON DAVIS on Lindsay Lohan

It doesn't matter how gym-toned the girl might be, there is still something about her that looks like she was designed to bring in the washing.

JENNY ECLAIR on Coleen Rooney

She'll never be as big as me – look at her nose and her boobs, she's ugly.

JORDAN on Jody Marsh

I think she's worth about seven million [dollars], which means she's really poor. It's disgusting. She lives in a motel.

BRANDON DAVIS on Lindsay Lohan

This is one Hilton that should be closed for renovation.

MR BLACKWELL on Paris Hilton